James M. Lauderdale

Letters to the peers of Scotland

James M. Lauderdale

Letters to the peers of Scotland

ISBN/EAN: 9783743341791

Manufactured in Europe, USA, Canada, Australia, Japa

Cover: Foto ©ninafisch / pixelio.de

Manufactured and distributed by brebook publishing software (www.brebook.com)

James M. Lauderdale

Letters to the peers of Scotland

TO THE

PEERS OF SCOTLAND.

BY THE

EARL OF LAUDERDALE.

LONDON:

PRINTED FOR G. G. AND J. ROBINSON,
PATERNOSTER-ROW.

MDCCXCIV.

INTRODUCTION.

THERE is no subject which has more exercised the ingenuity of those who have thus intruded on the public, than the framing of what might appear an adequate apology for the presumption it exhibits.

I am perfectly conscious that ambition of applause is the motive to which such an attempt will be generally attributed, and that in the mind of moſt, its failure, as in ſimilar caſes, will be attended with a degree of contempt proportionable to the ſuppoſed exorbitance of the expectation of the man who preſumes to addreſs them; and I can aſſure you, that my experience of the extent of the goodnature and indulgence of men on theſe ſubjects, and the little practice I have had of arranging or ſtating my thoughts in writing, would have prevented me from addreſſing theſe letters to you, and ſtill more, from ſubjecting them to the public eye, at any other period than in times ſuch as thoſe in which we live.

But whilſt the induſtry with which

calumnies

calumnies have been circulated, renders, in my apprehenſion, an explanation of my motives to you neceſſary; an attempt by a plain and ſimple ſtatement to bring back to the recollection of the nation the various ſteps by which folly, art, and miſmanagement have combined to miſlead the public mind, and to ſink the country into its preſent ſtate of calamity, cannot be diſadvantageous to them: and if it exhibits in its imperfections a proof of my want of ability, I ſhall in my own mind feel ample compenſation, if it produces in yours the conviction that I am ready to hazard any thing rather than that my public conduct ſhould not ſtand fairly in your eſtimation.

The impreſſion which fine words make is one thing, and the conviction of reaſon another; I have no habits of compoſition, and if I had, I have not vanity ſufficient to ſuppoſe that I could miſlead you into an approbation of that which appeared to myſelf culpable. But, convinced of the rectitude of my conduct, it is not by art I wiſh to court your approbation, but by reaſon to command it; and in attempting to effect this, I look forward with confidence, that the ſtrength of the caſe, brought under view at a moment when prejudice has in ſome degree ſubſided, will ſink in your minds the imperfections of the ſtatement.

In relying on the nature of the times as an apology for my intrufion, I mean not to allude to any of thofe misfortunes, fo often dwelt upon, which are the univerfal attendants of warfare; nor to thofe themes of complaint which, though often true, have been generally malicioufly regarded as the refort of difappointed politicians. The fcenes of unparalleled difafters, that have followed one another with unprecedented rapidity, appropriate in the minds of all, characteriftic calamities to the times; and there are none who have attended to the periodical publications of the day, who muft not have obferved, that a fyftem of fcandalous infinuation and difgraceful ca-

lumny

lumny has been carried on by men
fuppofed to be under the influence of
Government, and who have undoubtedly by them been fcreened from the
juftice of their country *, as novel in
itfelf,

---

* The following libel, amongſt many others, appeared about a year ago, in a paper called The True
Briton.

" How filently the rogues of London have paffed
" over the fwindling and fraudulous tricks of the con-
" ventional rogues of Paris! They have not applauded
" the meafures of confifcating the property of ftrangers
" in the public funds in France, and they dare not con-
" demn it. In the one cafe they would be hooted at, and
" fpurned by every honeſt man in the kingdom; and
" in the fecond, they would lofe their falaries; and
" which by the by they are likely to do very foon; for
" Danton has publicly declared that no confidence is to
" be placed in the Engliſh at Paris, who call themfelves
" the victims of the Britiſh Government; and that they
" ought

itself, as it is disgraceful to the age. If therefore a sense of the first, which is, now

" ought all to be imprisoned. Lord Kenyon appears to
" be of the same opinion in some cases that have come
" before him; and the Traitors, who would have sacri-
" ficed their country to France, are now very properly
" punished by being renounced by both. O ye Priest-
" leys! Ye Frosts! Ye Stones! Ye Paines! Ye Sir
" Robert Smiths! and ye Lauderdales! What say you
" to this opinion of Danton, and the loss of your pro-
" perty?—You have neither character nor consideration
" in France or England:—despised in the latter, and
" spurned by the former, where will ye seek refuge?"

Upon applying to the Attorney General for proof of the publication, I was by him with great civility and attention informed, that he had no authority over the officers employed to purchase the newspapers; he referred me however to the Treasury, and stated, with that certainty which his idea of justice and propriety suggested, his conviction that I would there get that which on a similar application had been granted to others.

But

now pretty generally felt, can vindicate in your minds the attempt I am about to make, I should flatter myself that none can abstain from sympathizing with the desire I feel, by fair and plain explanation, of doing away the

But after a long evasive correspondence with the Secretary of the Treasury, though he acknowledged its having been granted in several cases, some of which he named, I found I could not even learn from him the mode in which my application should be made.

In this dilemma I wrote to Mr. Pitt himself, and, by his directions, laid my request before the Board in the shape of a Memorial, which was by them immediately negatived.—The whole correspondence is now in my possession.

I perfectly well know the assiduity with which the report has been circulated, of my possessing property in France, and even encouraged by those who I believe must have been as much convinced of the falsehood of it as myself.

effect

effect which may have been unjustly produced by the last.

Various are the modes to which the art and ambition of Ministers have resorted, as means of obtaining or retaining their situations. But it was reserved for this Administration to endeavour to secure their ill-got power, by coupling the existence of the government of the country with their own existence in office; to treat, with unparalleled presumption, opposition to them, even if conducted by means formerly practised by themselves *, as rebellion

---

* See the Preamble to the Duke of Richmond's Bill, and his Letter to Lieutenant Colonel Sharman; the
Resolutions

rebellion against the state; to hold out the continuance of their measures as the only security for the government of the country, and the moment of their downfall as the sure æra of a revolution. To establish this belief through the medium of their own superior merit or management, has long appeared, even to themselves, impracticable;—but they have stooped, by calumny and insinuation, to endeavour to create a misrepresentation of the motives of others, and thus have looked to the diffidence which, by art, they could create in the minds of the public, of the principles of their op-

Resolutions at the Thatched House Tavern, where Mr. Pitt was present; and his Speeches on Reform.

ponents,

ponents, as the source of that security which the knowledge of their own merits made them despair of acquiring, by attempting to establish a confidence in themselves,

It is to do away any impression which their industry in this pursuit may have made, that, in the following letters, I wish to disclose to you the real motives that have actuated a man who, on the subject of the present war, has been a uniform opposer of their measures; to unveil to you the disguised motives of those who have contributed to involve the nation in it; and to exhibit to you that series of unsystematic mismanagement, which, as it will account

count for the calamities that are paſt, will teach you what you have to expect in future.

By theſe means I hope, if it has been any where ſuccefsfully eſtabliſhed, to diſlodge the prejudice, that there is any thing in common betwixt the power and the meaſures of thoſe who now manage the affairs of the country, and the exiſtence of our happy Conſtitution.

The attempt is that which ought to be as grateful to the Sovereign as to his People; for if the love of the Conſtitution, univerſally prevalent, makes the public voice anxiouſly ex-
preſs

press its desire of perpetuating the blessings which from it they derive, the Sovereign and his Family have under it too deep a stake, I trust in God too permanent a one, to wish to see its existence coupled, even in idea, with that of any administration; far less with that of an administration who by their measures have brought themselves into such a situation, that they can neither advance without ruin, nor retreat without disgrace.

LETTERS, &c.

LETTER I.

AS the numerous publications that have at various periods appeared, on the origin and progrefs of the French Revolution, are admitted by all to have contributed much to the amufement and information of the public; fo it muft alfo be acknowledged, that this important fubject has been generally treated with a degree of talent that has juftly created a well-founded opinion of the capacity, and an admiration of the ingenuity, of thofe who have in this country

entered

entered at large into the confideration of it. No man can entertain a higher refpect than I do for the uncommon difplay of abilities that has been exhibited on this occafion; I fhould indeed conceive any wifh to detract from their merit as a mark of my own want of tafte and judgement. I muft however acknowledge, that I cannot reflect on the manner in which it has been difcuffed, or the point of view in which it has almoft been univerfally held out to our attention, without lofing in a confiderable degree the pleafure I derived from perufing them.

It might reafonably have been fuppofed that a great and fudden convulfion in a neighbouring kingdom would, in the firft inftance, have led to an inveftigation of the confequences it was likely to produce to our own country, and to the confideration of the line of conduct which it was prudent

and

and proper for us to purfue; and it would have perhaps been fortunate, if, inftead of launching into the wide fea of its univerfal operation, they had limited themfelves to the narrow view of its effects in our national fecurity; if, inftead of inveftigating its connection with the general interefts of man, and the ftate of happinefs or mifery it was likely to diffufe over the world, the writers of this country had confined themfelves more immediately to its connection with the interefts of Englifhmen, and the profperity of this nation. The fubject, even in this point of view, feemed to furnifh ample ground for fpeculation. The deftruction of a government whofe monarchs and ftatefmen had fo often difturbed the tranquillity of this country, and facrificed the peace of Europe to that reftlefs fpirit of ambition and political intrigue, with which experience had taught us that they had for upwards of a century been uniformly animated, was in itself deeply interesting, and the consequences of it to us could not fail to appear to all sufficiently important.

But, dazzled with the greatness of the scene, and the magnitude of the questions agitated in the exalted imaginations of those who have treated on the subject, the narrow views of national interest and national security have been eclipsed. Every question relative to the organization of the internal government of France has been considered as intimately connected with the general interests of mankind, and the immediate happiness of the universe. Lost to the recollection of all national feeling, or perhaps looking with contempt on the possession of it, —as citizens of the world, they have stepped forward to the contest with all the prejudices of citizens of France they have generally terminated in conducting it.

An

An admirer however of that wifdom which diftinguifhed the conduct of M. de Vergennes, who, at the commencement of our conteft with America, anxioufly courted the attention of the learned and ingenuous of his country, to the inveftigation of the confequences that were likely to refult to France and Spain from the ftruggle; and left us to difcufs amongft ourfelves the abftract queftions concerning the due limits of that filial affection which might be expected from a colony, or the extent of that right of taxation for which we contended;—it will be my object in this letter, alone to draw your attention to the Revolution of France, as it has affected the political fituation of this country.

A uniform opponent of that fyftem of conduct which has been adopted, I fhall, by purfuing this inquiry, have an opportunity of of displaying to you the real grounds on which I have acted—of subjecting to your view the motives which, in the discussion of the important questions that have presented themselves for decision, have regulated my conduct—and I shall have thus the satisfaction of thinking, that, if I should unfortunately meet with your disapprobation, that disapprobation will arise from a fair difference of opinion, and not from any prejudice created by those libellous insinuations, with which it is the fashion of the day to assail those who wish to build their opinions upon the sound foundation of reason uninfluenced by temporary alarms, or who have not yet learned to make their public conduct uniformly subservient to their private views of interest.

The Revolution in France, whilst no one yet seemed alive to the idea that the immediate interests of this country would be affected by it, had attracted the attention of all:—by the discerning in France it had long, from the situation of that country, been foreseen; but in this—where we were not likely to derive any information from the intercourse of our Government with its Court, who were interested to conceal the situation; nor from our travellers, who in general associated with the Clergy and Nobility, a class of men that appear to have remained blind to their situation to the last—it came upon us by surprise: and if the event itself was unexpected, the mode in which it was conducted was no less so. The energy and vigour displayed in the proceedings of the States General, the resolution and firmness which distinguished their measures, contrasted with that levity and frivolity which the nation had formerly exhibited, and which we we had long conceived to be the chief feature in their character, whilst it augmented the surprise, naturally added to the interest which was universally felt in the struggle; and there existed none who did not see with astonishment—many who viewed with admiration—the great and animated exertions of a people contending for what all, of necessity, regarded as the object of the greatest importance that could occupy the mind of man.

Whilst it thus gratified by its novelty, and interested the speculations of those who had made the mind of man, the progress of society, and the nature of government, the subject of abstract investigation—it afforded to the politician, who considered only the situation of this country, matter of joy and exultation. The extinction of a government, whose restless spirit of intrigue, whose continued love of warfare, whatever might be the character of the monarch on the throne, or the statesmen that surrounded him, promised to the nations of Europe the enjoyment of more peace and tranquillity than they had hitherto possessed; to us, in particular, the benefits that seemed likely to attend it were great. We daily felt the advantages of the increase of our capital, arising from that transfer of moveable property which always has, and which always will take place, from a country in a state of revolution, to that country the tranquillity of whose government seems to afford the greatest prospect of security. In the circumstances which attended the internal arrangements in which France was engaged, we saw what we thought constituted the impossibility of any attack being made on her part for years: in anticipating the peace and tranquillity we were likely thus to enjoy, we began to perceive the rapid diminution of that national debt with which we were loaded, and which forms the only check upon the enterprising spirit of the nation: in anticipating that which the other nations of Europe were likely to enjoy, we saw the extension of our commerce by the increased demand of our manufactures, upon which we knew our wealth, our prosperity, and our importance as a nation, ultimately to depend.

Our hopes of security rested not alone upon the destruction of the old government of France: the hatred and detestation in which all the principles that had actuated it were held by those who seemed to succeed to the management of the government of that country, afforded us well-grounded hopes that innovations would not be confined to arrangements in her interior government; it in a degree confirmed the reasonable expectation, which we formed, of seeing a change in that

that syſtem which ſhe had long purſued in her intercourſe with foreign nations, not leſs beneficial to herſelf, than it was likely to be to the reſt of Europe.

The language too which upon all occaſions ſhe uſed, the ſentiments which at firſt diſtinguiſhed all her public acts, as they ſpoke an averſion to hoſtilities, a deſire of cultivating the arts of peace, tended not a little to eſtabliſh that opinion of the advantage to be derived from the change, which general reaſoning had taught us to think we were likely to enjoy.

Such were the happy proſpects entertained by almoſt all;—by thoſe who judged from the documents that were in the hands of every one—by thoſe whoſe ſituation might be ſuppoſed to give them acceſs to preferable ſources of information—by the philoſopher,

losopher who, in his closet, viewed with pleasure the advantages which mankind were likely to derive from the existence of a free government, over a people who had long laboured under a pressure of laws and regulations, with which the vicious ambition, the folly and the ignorance of its old government had loaded it—as well as by the practical politician, who, in the senate, announced with eagerness the advantages which we as a nation were likely to derive from the change; and whilst in the pulpit we heard it employ the eloquence of Dr. Price, in the House of Commons it commanded the exertions of Mr. Pitt, who, alluding to it in his memorable speech on the finances of the country, in February 1792, declared, " That unquestionably there never was a " time when, from the situation of Europe, " we might more reasonably expect fifteen " years of peace than we may at the present " moment."

With

With what aftonifhment will he, who at a future period reads the hiftory of the day, fee, within a few pages, all thefe profpects of peace and fecurity vanifh before his eye!—With what aftonifhment muft every one retrace in his recollection, that though it is little more than two years fince the declaration was made, this country has been engaged, for near a year and a half, in one of the moft expenfive and difaftrous wars of which our hiftory affords us any recollection—has been with induftry employed, by remonftrances, intrigues and fubfidies, in endeavouring to engage every European power in the conflict—and in purfuing a fyftem that none ever held out more ftrongly as deftructive to our interefts, than thofe who have been the promoters and conductors of it!

That it has been entered into with the approbation of the public, is a thing which cannot

cannot be difputed; but it ought always to be recollected, that as national character is moulded and framed from the form of the government under which we live—as the penfivenefs or levity which diftinguifhes individuals, the nature of the inveftigations in which they are led to occupy their minds, the characteriftics of the refults which they are induced to form, depend much on the government and inftitutions under which they live—fo it is in the power of all governments to communicate temporary impreffions, and in general for a time to guide the minds of the people over whom they prefide;—and perhaps there has been no period when more pains were taken, by alarms, by mifreprefentation and defamation, to affect the public mind, and reconcile it to the fyftem which has been purfued.

Taught to value the bleffings of peace, by the experience of the benefit during

thefe

these last ten years we have derived from it, by the unparalleled situation and prosperity we had attained; still alive to the recollection of the calamities which had attended a perseverance in the American war, and the ruin in which by it we had well nigh been involved; having imbibed pretty generally, from the speculations of the enlightened age in which we live, an opinion that hardly any success, or the attainment of any object we could imagine to ourselves, could compensate to us as a nation for the certain calamities of war; viewing, in the interruption of our commerce, in the expence in which we inevitably must be involved, certain and sure misfortunes which no acquisition of foreign territory could counterbalance or repay; it was no light and trivial reason, it was no moderate fermentation of opinion, that could have insured a patient hearing for any one who

proposed

proposed to involve us in hostilities; and nothing short of the hope of being able to convince the nation that it was necessary for its existence, seemed to afford any prospect of its being universally relished.

To produce these effects no exertion was neglected, by every insinuation and management. The belief was impressed on our minds, that the balance of power in Europe, for which we had so often contended, was destroyed; that our allies, whom we were in honour and interest bound to defend, were about to be sacrificed to a degree of ambition, of the extent of which, even the recollection of Lewis the Fourteenth could furnish us with no idea; and lastly, that that constitution under which we enjoyed happiness and prosperity, and which almost all equally agreed in admiring, was about to be undermined. The horrors committed

by

by the French, whilst the pressure of external foes, and the real grounds from which they had originated, were kept out of sight, were anxiously brought forward to rouse the passions, and by prejudice to bar in our thoughts every idea of the possibility of treating. By our fears and our hopes we were alternately assailed and flattered; and the number of visionary republicans in this country, ready to co-operate in the destruction of our constitution, were represented to us as alone to be equalled by the number of imaginary royalists in France, who were ready to join us upon our first appearance in the field; and whilst the consideration of the strength, of the great military skill and experience of the powers with whom we were about to co-operate, flattered us, on the Continent, with speedy and splendid success to be attained at no very immoderate expence, we were taught to look-for-

ward

ward with avidity to the profpect of mercantile advantage, which the deftruction of the naval power of France, and the poffeffion of her colonies would afford.

Such were the opinions that induftry and power combined fuccefsfully to propagate; and it became the creed of all, that as war was the fure means of extending our confequence and importance abroad, fo at home it was the only one of fecuring peace and tranquillity, and of preferving that conftitution which we had all fuch an intereft in maintaining; in the prefervation of peace, in the idea of obtaining redrefs or fecurity by treaty, were every where difcovered the feeds of external calamity, and of internal convulfion.—To doubt, to hefitate, far more to advance an opinion to the contrary, was to fubject yourfelf to the charge, and even in the ideas of many to furnifh proof complete, of connections with the enemies of of the country abroad, and with secret fomenters of sedition at home.

Time and experience have now, in a degree, dispelled all those confused conceptions of imaginary success, which so universally floated in the minds of the people of this country;—the events on the Continent; the enormity of the expence already with certainty anticipated; the extent of the taxes which must be laid on; the consideration of the loss of property and restraint of liberty, which accumulation of taxes always produces, have roused pretty generally doubts of the expediency of war; but in the mouths of almost all, if not in their minds, peace is still stigmatized as likely to be productive of every possible evil; and the real calamities which we see and feel from war, are dogmatically represented as likely to be exceeded by those which we imagine will at-

tend,

tend, or which, perhaps as a sacrifice to our consistency, we obstinately attribute to peace.

Before this change took place, to have attempted any explanation of my motives, any vindication of my conduct, with hopes of success, would have been foolish and absurd; nay, even now I am diffident whether the advocate for peace—he who sees in war no possible advantage, and every species of calamity; he who from experience regards our perseverance in it as the sure method of nourishing and creating internal sedition and convulsion; as the undoubted means of degrading us as a nation, and sinking our relative consequence amongst the powers of Europe—can flatter himself with meeting amongst the public many who will peruse with an impartial eye what he may be disposed to state; or who will not rest satisfied, when the nature of the attempt

here

here dawns upon them, with anticipating the abſurdity of his arguments, and prejudging the wickedneſs of his concluſion.

From you, however, whoſe partiality I have experienced, whoſe liberality of ſentiment I know, I truſt for favour, and flatter myſelf I indulge no ill-grounded expectation, in hoping that I ſhall be enabled to engage your attention to a ſhort inveſtigation into the nature of the Revolution in France, and a conſideration of the effects which the line of conduct we have purſued, and are purſuing in conſequence of it, has had upon this country; as well as to what probably would have been the conſequence of our ſteadily endeavouring to perſevere in that ſyſtem of neutrality which we adopted on the firſt appearance of it, and that predilection for peace which at that time manifeſted itſelf in our conduct. In doing this it is my intention in this letter, to conſider the nation as without party, and to view them as if with unanimity they had adopted the one or the other line.

It has been in general the happiness of those who speculate upon, and still more of those who are called to conduct the affairs of a great nation, that events, however important and extraordinary in themselves, are seldom so completely issolated; so wide of the usual range of speculation, or unlike any thing that the page of history records, as to deprive us, in the investigations that lead to the forming of those opinions necessary for the regulation of our conduct, of that benefit which we acquire from the experience of others; of that surest of all guidances which we derive from avoiding the errors, and adopting that which has proved itself by events to be the wisdom of those who have preceded us. There are, however,

however, many things which diftinguifh the French Revolution; perhaps fome that form the moft remarkable and important features of it, fo novel in themfelves, fo unlike any thing with which the hiftory of man renders us familiar, as to force the politician, in meafuring the fteps that it is fit to purfue, to have recourfe exclufively to general principles, without which, undoubtedly, the application of the fkill of no one can be perfect, and which, aided by practical experience, is what alone enables him to come to fure and definite conclufions.

Many are the convulfions, numerous indeed are the revolutions, with which the annals of the world make us converfant;—acts of perfonal oppreffion of individuals; the ambition of chiefs; the ftruggles of contending parties; the jealoufies of the various or-

ders

ders in the community; the proud oppreffions of elated monarchs, with all their confequences, have but too often extended their baneful influence over the different nations with which hiftory has rendered us acquainted. We all recollect the events that followed the violated chaftity of Lucretia; the judicial murder of a Horne and an Egmont, and the firm and noble refiftance made to acts of extortion by a Hampden. We cannot forget the generous ftruggles for liberty which diftinguifh the hiftory of our own country, and the ultimate expulfion of its monarchs. But in vain fhall we confult our memories, in vain fhall we attempt in retracing hiftory, to difcover the features of a nation that had exifted for centuries under a form of government, in which we had been taught to believe that it had long habitually prided itfelf; where, without any inftance of immediate active oppreffion

that

that drew forth refiftance; without any act of tyranny on the part of the monarch; nay, with a general belief, even in his enemies, of his goodnefs; without any ftruggle amongft the different orders of the ftate; all feemed to agree in the neceffity of fuch alterations as virtually amounted to *a diffolution of its exifting government*. Yet he who looks at the fituation of France, who reads with attention the numerous addreffes of its parliaments, the accounts of the enthufiafm with which they were received by the people, who examines the propofitions entertained by the Nobility in the Affembly of the Notables, and the Addrefs propofed by the Bifhop of Blois, which was agreed to and prefented by the Clergy, cannot abftain from admitting, that all orders of the community feemed to affent to this *propofition*. Nay, the fchemes of innovation, to the extent of alteration of what had long been its practical constitution, successively brought forward by its Ministers, shewed a conviction, even on the part of those who managed the government, of the necessity of a change. The Assemblée des Notables of M. de Calonne, the Cours Plenier of MM. de Brienne and Lamoignon, the calling together the States General by M. Neckar, were all successive proofs of the opinion of those Ministers. And the Court, in the edict for assembling the States General, which gave to the Tiers Etats a number equal to the other two orders, seemed not only to pronounce the necessity of the extinction of the government that existed in practice, but to declare the inadequacy (to the situation of the times) of those checks and institutions, which existed in France at a former period.

There

There were few who confidered its lingering exiftence, that did not forefee in the calling together the States General, the death warrant of the exifting government of France, and who did not look to the period of their meeting, as fubftantially the moment of its diffolution. There was none who did not perceive, foon after they were affembled, that the practical government of the country, which had long exifted, and under which the character of the nation had been formed, and the habits of individuals contracted, was annihilated; who did not view with aftonifhment the little refiftance with which its diffolution was effected; who could regard in any other light, than as in a manner the operation of magic, the deftruction of that Baftille which had been for ages the dread of France; the defection of that army, whofe attachment to their monarch had been the theme of the world; and the affumption of the powers of government by a National Affembly, of the exiftence of which the hiftory of their country furnifhes not the moft remote precedent.

New and extraordinary as this phænomenon may appear, unaccountable as at firft fight it may feem, we may trace its origin to circumftances from whence it muft have naturally proceeded, to caufes however, which being themfelves novel in their nature, never could exhibit their effects till the age in which we live.

The fyftem of providing for the extraordinary expences of a government, by mortgaging the public revenues, is an invention of a modern date;—the treafures feized by Julius in Rome, during the civil wars; thofe poffeffed by the different Grecian republics;

the immenfe fums amaffed by the fucceffors of Alexander, fufficiently fhew the prudent practice of antiquity, in providing in the time of peace and tranquillity for thofe expences which might be neceffary in the moment of public exigency.

From ancient hiftory, we can therefore derive no experience of the confequences which attend carrying to excefs that funding fyftem firft introduced by fome of the modern Italian ftates, and which in this century has been carried by our own, as well as other European nations, to fo alarming an extent. In modern times, the confequences of it had been the fubject of much ingenious fpeculation amongft the learned, but we poffeffed no practical experience that could make us acquainted with the extent of the evils with which it might be connected;—the rapid progrefs of commerce and manufactures,

tures, the increasing prosperity and accumulated wealth which attended them amongst the nations that carried this system the furthest, had enabled them, by a gradual increase of taxes, to palliate the mischiefs that seemed to flow from it, and in a degree to arrest the disorder in its progress. We had witnessed, indeed, many of the evils connected with its slighter symptoms, even on our own robust constitution; but the fatal effects of the more advanced stages of the disorder upon the weakly frame of the French government, presented a new scene to our view. The eyes of all had been long opened to the fallacy of that fanciful sophistry, that saw in public incumbrances, the riches and the wealth of the people who contracted them, that viewed them as useful engines for promoting the commerce and prosperity of the nation in which they existed; but the extent of the evil, the ultimate

mate confequences, which it was likely to produce, could be accurately limited or defined in the fpeculation of none. Even the experience of what had happened under one form of government, if it had exifted, would have afforded no conclufion, that could have enabled us, with precifion, to infer what might be the event in another. For if on the one hand it appeared clear that the fyftem might be continued, and the load of debt augmented, as long as the ingenuity of the financier could render palatable, or the government enforce the payment of thofe taxes which it made neceffary; fo, on the other, it was obvious that the extent of his fkill muft of neceffity be regulated by the opulence or poverty of the community, over whofe affairs he prefided; and, that the power to enforce, muft depend upon the nature of the inftitutions and government of that country in which the fyftem was adopted.

adopted.—"Our popular government," fays Mr. Hume, " perhaps will render it diffi-
" cult or dangerous for a Minifter to venture
" on fo defperate an expedient as that of
" a voluntary bankruptcy. And though
" the Houfe of Lords be altogether com-
" pofed of proprietors of land, and the
" Houfe of Commons chiefly; and confe-
" quently neither of them can be fuppofed
" to have great property in the funds; yet,
" the connection of the members may be
" fo great with the proprietors, as to render
" them more tenacious of public faith, than
" prudence, policy, or even juftice, ftrictly
" fpeaking, requires; and perhaps too, our
" foreign enemies may be fo politic as to
" difcover that our fafety lies in defpair,
" and may not therefore fhew the danger,
" open and barefaced, till it be inevitable.
" The balance of power in Europe, our
" grand-fathers, our fathers, and we, have
" all

" all deemed too unequal to be preserved
" without our attention and assistance:—*but
" our children, weary of the struggle, and
" fettered with incumbrances, may sit down
" secure, and see their neighbours oppressed
" and conquered, till at last they themselves,
" and their creditors, lie both at the mercy of
" the conqueror; and this, properly enough,
" be denominated the violent death of our
" public credit.*"

But in making this conjecture, Mr. Hume could alone have reference to a government in which the nature of its political institutions had led to the burthens being equally spread over all, and in which the resources had been, by that means, fairly exhausted. Had he contemplated a nation, where the financier was hampered with privileges, and hemmed in on all sides with

absurd

absurd exemptions, whose government and political institutions were so weakened with the monopolies and privileges with which it was inseparably interwoven, as not to possess vigour and energy within itself to get rid of them, however conscious the whole community avowed themselves of the necessity of it; then he would probably have formed to himself a very different conclusion. He would have seen the government of such a country, not as likely to fall a prey to foreign enemies; he would not have viewed it at the feet of a conqueror, but he would have described it as likely to fall a sacrifice to the belief of its incapacity which uniformly pervaded the community.

If in the evils attending this new system of providing for the wants of the state, we can trace the cause of this extraordinary event, our wonder and surprise at the facility and eafe with which it was effected will alfo in a degree vanifh; when we confider the enormity of the evil under which France laboured, and which its government had myfterioufly concealed till the annual extent of the defalcation of the revenue was fo great, that the dread of the increafing difficulties which it forefaw, could on the one hand no longer permit it to palliate; and on the other, in its cramped, weak, and enervated ftate, it was equally unfit to meet the creditor with a refufal, or the public with a demand.

He whofe habits of vice and diffipation have brought ruin upon himfelf, when reduced to diftrefs, may take to the highway; but in attempting to get forcibly the pittance with which he means to purchafe his daily bread, a ftruggle will enfue: the merchant whofe fuppofed opulence has fecured an extenfive

tenfive credit, though he may have long known the fituation of his affairs, though he may have forefeen that he was about to involve hundreds in ruin, when the hour of bankruptcy comes, difappears from the Exchange, and is permitted quietly to retreat.

The neceffities of the court of Charles the Firft, to adminifter to its momentary expences, induced them to attempt forcibly the levying of illegal exactions; hiftory informs us of the ftruggle that enfued. The neceffities of the court of Lewis the Sixteenth, occafioned by the embarraffment in a great and complicated fyftem of finance in which it was involved, when the hour of reckoning came, exhibited to mankind a ftriking proof that the Exchange is not the moft important fituation from whence, in the moment of fimilar calamity, a quiet and peaceable retreat may be made. Betwixt the

the affairs of individuals and national concerns, there is always some resemblance, some analogy, to be traced.

Though the causes are various to which you may attribute the scenes that immediately followed the dissolution of the old government;—though that love of liberty which instantly shone forth and discovered itself, and which seemed to guide at first all their proceedings, may be traced as arising from the general diffusion of knowledge which prevailed, from the habits of admiring the effects of freedom, which even the Court itself had endeavoured to excite, when in America, as in Holland, it protected the cause of democracy; and from writings on the subject, which, during that period, had been not only permitted but encouraged;—yet it is to the operation of the excess of this funding system on the

vicious

vicious frame of the French Monarchy, which you may exclusively attribute the diffolution of the old government, and its perfect incapacity to proceed. For if we were for a moment to fancy that greater energy had been difplayed in its defence, that the armed force which furrounded Paris had been brought to act, and that the Affembly had by their means been difmiffed, there is no one who can think, that, when it had difgufted the people at large, perhaps embrued its hands in their blood, that government would have poffeffed influence fufficient to extricate itfelf from difficulties which it antecedently had not courage to face.

There is no one can reafonably conjecture that this would have had any other effect than retarding the hour of the calamity, or perhaps accelerating thofe fcenes

of

of horror which mankind have since had so much reason to regret.

France now exhibited a new scene to the eyes of mankind, the first great victim to the rash and improvident management of this modern system of Finance. We saw, not in an infant nation, but amongst a people, who, in spite of the drawback under which they had laboured from the nature of their government, had stood the foremost in civilization, and in the cultivation of the arts and sciences, every trace of its government destroyed. We saw all the political institutions of a nation palsied and annihilated, who are well described by a modern Philosopher, when he says, " The French are the only people, " except the Greeks, who have been at " once Philosophers, Poets, Orators, Histo-" rians, Painters, Architects, Sculptors, and " Musicians.

" Muficians. With regard to the Stage
" they had excelled even the Greeks, who
" far excelled the Englifh; and in common
" life they have in a great meafure perfect-
" ed that Art, the moſt ufeful and agree-
" able of any, *l'Art de vivre,* the Art of So-
" ciety and Converfation."

The bufy fcenes in which the people of
France were of neceffity about to be engaged,
were but too likely to carry them on in the
progrefs, naturally dictated by the fituation
in which the diffolution of the old government left them. But the fpeculation of what
was likely to enfue did not alone concern
them; it required not much forefight to
difcover how much it was interefting to the
reſt of the world—how much, in particular,
it was interefting to us, who had long been
accuſtomed to confider that country as a
rival.

It was a subject that demanded the utmost attention, as it required the most enlarged talents in our statesmen.—It called for the exercise of those talents which qualify men for taking a lead in the uncommon and more important situations of society; there was here no precedent that could be called in, no official experience that could aid or assist; " for, when the high roads are " broken up and the waters out, when a " new and troubled scene is opened, and " the file affords no precedent; then it is " that a greater knowledge of mankind is " requisite than office ever gave, or than " office ever can give."

In pursuing this investigation, the path was not however barren; there were many things that tended to aid and assist the mind;—for though deprived of any experience of a nation, which directly or even

remotely

remotely refembled in its fituation that of France, the confideration of the manners, of the habits, and of the character of the different claffes of individuals that formed the community, feemed to prefent to us grounds on which to build our fpeculations.

France, indeed, had loft its government; but the people of France had not, could not, fhake off thofe different modifications of character which under it they had acquired. We ftill faw diftinctly remaining the various claffes of the community to which the nature of the old inftitutions had given rife;—we ftill faw exifting in each the habits, the diftinguifhing characteriftics, with which the vice or the weaknefs of the ancient government had ftamped them.

We faw in the nobility and clergy that were ufed to furround the throne, a clafs of men corrupted and debased by the mode in which they had been educated; by the manner in which they had lived; whose fortunes had fallen a victim to the enormous extravagance encouraged by the Court, and who had been subsequently maintained in their luxurious habits by the corrupt profusion of it; and in that description of those two orders, who, remote from the Court, lived in the different provinces, we beheld men practiced in the exercise of that little village-tyranny, which their superiority had authorized; accustomed to enjoy those exemptions and privileges on which they habitually prided themselves, and which taught them to regard those beneath them as almost a different class of beings *.

We

---

* In the *Cahiers* of the nobility, at the time of the States General, we find them steadily demanding, that all their feudal rights should be confirmed: that the carrying of arms should be strictly prohibited to every body,

We saw in those who composed the different Parliaments a proud magistracy, who, though their ambition and the necessities of the state had led them every where to oppose the fiscal oppressions of the Court, loved the consequence they enjoyed, and looked with satisfaction at that exclusive privilege of administering justice or injustice

body, but noblemen: that the infamous arrangements of the militia should remain on its old footing: that breaking up parks, and inclosing commons, should be prohibited: that the nobility alone should be eligible to enter into the army, church, &c. that lettres de cachet should continue: that the press should not be free: and in fine, that there should be no free corn trade. Those of the clergy maintain that the liberty of the press ought rather to be restrained than extended: that the laws against it should be renewed and executed: that admission into religious orders should be, as formerly, at sixteen years of age: that lettres de cachet are useful, and even necessary. They solicit to prohibit all division of commons, and to revoke the edict allowing inclosures.

over

over his people which they had purchased from the Sovereign.

In the middling orders of society we saw many, who had acquired affluence by the commerce in which they had been engaged, averse to the old system, from the restraints which, by its improvident laws, they had laboured under in the conduct of their profession,—as well as from a recollection of the little personal estimation in which, under it, they were held.—In this class we also found the disciples of Voltaire, Rousseau, Mably, Turgot, and the economists, a set of men, the pupils of those who had enlightened the world with their speculations; amongst whom the principles of political economy had been long better understood, and more thoroughly digested, than they were in any other nation; who had by their various publications tinged the mind of the

whole

whole community with an idea of liberty which their habits rendered them incapable of digeſting.

In the lower orders, which bore in numbers an infinitely greater proportion to the others than it happily does in this country where property is diffuſed, we ſaw human nature in an abject ſituation indeed! a people devoid of all property, who looked alone to the labour of their hands for their daily ſupport, and who were in many inſtances robbed of a great proportion of the pittance they could earn, that no encroachments might be made upon the exemptions and privileges of the other orders, in providing for the wants of the ſtate, and the luxuriant corruption of its court; a people rendered in their nature cruel, by the habitual want of feeling they had experienced on the part of their ſuperiors; and ſavage,

from

from the oppreſſion to which their minds had ſo long been trained *.

Such

* Though I could give many inſtances of the miſery of the lower orders in France from my own knowledge, and refer to eloquent paſſages in the works of the writers of that country, deſcriptive of the ſad ſituation to which they were reduced, I chooſe to confine myſelf to the following extracts from the works of Mr. Arthur Young, which, as they were recommended by Mr. Reeves and his aſſociation, may be ſuppoſed to furniſh that increaſed conviction the mind feels, when it extracts a fact from an unwilling witneſs.

Country-labour being 76 per cent. cheaper in France than in England, it may be inferred, that all thoſe claſſes which depend on labour, and are the moſt numerous in ſociety, are 76 per cent. leſs at their eaſe (if I may uſe the expreſſion), worſe fed, worſe cloathed, and worſe ſupported both in ſickneſs and in health, than the ſame claſſes in England, notwithſtanding the immenſe quantity of precious metals, and the impoſing appearance of wealth in France.

Walking up a long hill to eaſe my mare, I was joined by a poor woman, who complained of the times, and that

it

Such were the component parts of this great nation, who faw proftrate at their feet, from

it was a fad country; on my demanding her reafons, fhe faid, her hufband had but a morfel of land, one cow, and a poor little horfe, yet he had a franchar (42lb.) of wheat, and three chickens, to pay as a quit-rent to one feigneur; and four franchar of oats, one chicken, and 1 f. to pay to another, befide very heavy tailles and other taxes. She had feven children, and the cow's milk helped to make the foup. It was faid at prefent, that *fomething was to be done by fome great folks for fuch poor ones, but fhe did not know who or how*; but God *fend us better, car les tailles & les droits nous écrafent.* This woman at no great diftance might have been taken for fixty or feventy, her figure was fo bent, and her face fo furrowed and hardened by labour; but fhe faid, fhe was only twenty-eight. An Englifhman, who has not travelled, cannot imagine the figure made by infinitely the greater part of the country women in France; it fpeaks, at firft fight, hard and fevere labour; I am inclined to think, that they work harder than the men, and this, united with the more miferable labour of bringing a new race of flaves into the world, deftroys abfolutely all fymmetry of perfon, and every feminine appearance.

from the caufes I have detailed, without any great or proportionable exertion of their own, all

ance. To what are we to attribute this difference in the manners of the lower people in the two kingdoms? *To Government.*

The murder of a Seigneur, or a chateau in flames, is recorded in every newfpaper; the rank of the perfon who fuffers, attracts notice; but where do we find the regifter of that Seigneur's oppreffion of his pea-fantry, and his exactions of feudal fervices, from thofe whofe children were dying around them for want of bread? Where do we find the minutes that affigned thefe ftarving wretches to fome vile petty-fogger, to be fleeced by impofitions, and a mockery of juftice, in the feigneurial courts? Who gives us the awards of the in-tendant and his *fub-delegues,* which took off the taxes of a man of fafhion, and laid them with accumulated weight on the poor, who were fo unfortunate as to be his neighbours? Who has dwelt fufficiently upon ex-plaining all the ramification of defpotifm, regal, arifto-cratical, and ecclefiaftical, pervading the whole mafs of the people; reaching, like a circulating fluid, the

moft

all the laws and inftitutions under which they had lived.

What moft diftant capillary tubes of poverty and wretchednefs? In thefe cafes, the fufferers are too ignoble to be known, and the mafs too indifcriminate to be pitied.

What are we to think of demanding, as a favour, the permiffion——" *de nettoyer fes grains, de faucher les prés artificiels, & d'enlever fes chaumes fans égard pour la perdrix ou tout autre gibier?"——* An Englifh reader will fcarcely underftand it, without being told, that there were numerous edicts for preferving the game, which prohibited weeding and hoeing, left the young partridges fhould be difturbed; fleeping feed, left it fhould injure the game; manuring with night foil, left the flavour of the partridges fhould be injured by feeding on the corn fo produced; mowing hay, &c. before a certain time, fo late as to fpoil many crops; and taking away the ftubble, which would deprive the birds of fhelter.

BERRY.—*Argentan.*—They pay rent for a cottage 20 livres, get their fuel in the woods; their tailles 15 to 24 fous: as much for capitation, and do fix days labour in the roads.

ST.

What was to happen no one could accurately predict, it would have required the

ST. GEORGE.—They eat buck-wheat made in very thin cakes without leaven.

PELLECOY.—Poor women picking weeds into their aprons to feed their cows with, and something like this I have remarked, more or lefs, all the way from Calais; it conveys an idea of poverty and want of employment.

FALAISE.—Live very badly, much of the bread is barley and buck-wheat, and many have nothing elfe but this and water, unlefs cyder happens to be very cheap; their fuel what wood they can fteal.

MORLAIX to BREST.—The people of the country are all dreffed in great trowfers like breeches, many of them with naked legs, and moft with wooden fhoes; the women feemed from their perfons and features to be harder worked than horfes.

LYONS.—A room for a manufacturer 200 to 300 livres, and houfe rent of all forts very dear; 20,000 people are now (1790) ftarving: yet charities of all forts do not amount to lefs than a million of livres a year.

gift of prophecy, and far exceeds the narrow bounds of the intellect of man. To have foreseen the establishment of the Constitution of 1789;—the Revolution that ensued in August 1792;—the attempt to establish a republic, and to conduct the government by means of the intellectual powers alternately operating on the passions and the reason of man;—the subsequent dominion of anarchy, the cruelties that attended it;— and the extent of the emigrations that during these different changes would take place, was impossible.

But an analysis of the elements of which this society was formed, might have convinced any one, that to the debased minds of many incapable of bearing the sad reverse of fortune, of viewing the scenes which brought to their recollection their former power and splendour, emigration

would

would naturally prefent itfelf as a refource; —that if a government was to be formed by the joint efforts of the nobility and clergy that remained, and the middling orders whom the fcene had brought forward, it would naturally partake of a limited monarchy; that as the influence of name and nobility gradually difappeared, the efforts of the middling orders, from their averfion to any thing that approximated to the ancient fyftem, as well as from the nature of the opinions which in theory they had been accuftomed to hold, would make them relifh, and induce their leaders to attempt the eftablifhing a republic; and that, laftly, habituated to nothing but change, the paffions and ambition of the lower orders, broke loofe from all reftraint, fhould produce fomething like that extraordinary fcene of which we have all been witneffes.

The progress was natural, and, even if there had been no interference of external force, it seemed to flow from the nature and character of those who were unfortunately concerned, and the situation in which they were left. To anticipate the scenes of horror, which of necessity must have ensued in this last stage of the business, was that from which most would naturally revolt, but there were none who forced themselves to it that could reasonably doubt of the extent to which they would arrive.—The uninformed man who never saw power exercised, but with a view to the benefit of him who possessed it;—when he acquires it, regards it naturally as the privilege to play the tyrant. The cruelties and oppressions of men broke loose from the chains of power, are always in proportion to the weight of the chains with which they have been loaded. A mob in London generally

nerally terminates with the breaking of a few windows, or at most, with the destruction of a few houses. An insurrection amongst the negroes in the West Indies ends in the murder of the slave-drivers, too often in that of the planter's whole family.

We ought not, we cannot justly, ascribe to the new system those scenes which have so often disgusted us; to contemplate it is a task shocking to humanity; but constrained to it, the discerning eye discovers alone the natural consequences of the vicious absurdity of the old system. Its enormities afford a standard by which you may accurately commensurate the sad extent of the oppression over the poor, which under the ancient monarchy of France was exercised.

It is this reasoning, it is this analysis of the causes of the French Revolution, and of the horrors it has occafioned. It is the reflection, that there exifted in our finance the utmoft profperity, and with good management no chance of their getting into that ftate of diforder which produced the Revolution in France, that has always convinced me that there could be no natural tendency to a fimilar fituation in this country.

It is the conviction, that at all events the fcenes of that unrelenting love of blood that attended it, which feemed to be the legitimate offspring of its government, of thofe racks and Baftilles that it looked to, to fupport its power, never could be generated under the influence of the mild fpirit of our Laws, and the wife regulation of our Conftitution, which quieted all alarms in my mind upon that fubject.

It

It is this mode of confidering the fubject, however, that has long convinced me of the progreffive tendency that things had in France to the fituation in which they now are; and that would have led me—if I had thought that we could ever have a right to interfere in the internal regulations of another government, if I could have loft fight of that right which exifts in every community to form laws and inftitutions for its interior regulation, that principle upon which the independence of nations refts—if ever I could have forefeen the moment when views of expediency would have fanctioned the interference of this country for fuch a purpofe,—to applaud the wifdom of thofe who wifhed to call us into the field at an early period, to criticife the folly of thofe who put off interfering, till the moment in which this country took a part. To deftroy it at its birth might have been,

been, perhaps, an eafy, if a defirable tafk; we know what it is to cope with it when its giant ftrength has reached to maturity.

But the fyftem which this country wifely at firft purfued, permitted it not to think that it could have a right, that the time could ever arrive when it would be expedient, to interfere.

In the moft authentic and folemn mode in which the opinions of thofe who conducted the government could be declared, in his Majefty's fpeeches from the Throne, we had the happinefs to fee the right of interference difclaimed; the expediency of it reprobated; the profpect of our continuing in peace held out with fatisfaction; and the hope of the general peace of Europe, wifely ftated to us as a commercial nation, as if it

deeply

deeply concerned our interests. In its increasing riches the country felt the benefit of this conduct; in the happiness which they enjoyed, the people felt the blessings of it; in the tendency which it had to preserve in the minds of foreign powers that idea of consequence we had acquired by our struggle against so many nations during the latter period of the American war, mankind saw the policy of it; the nation universally marked it with their approbation, and they were apparently as unanimous for maintaining it as ever they have been for the war—in reality much more so.

That system has been however abandoned; and, at a late period, we have been plunged into a war, the object of which, as the fermentation of the public opinion seemed likely to sympathize with it, has successively been stated:—first, to be the security

curity of Holland, the maintenance of treaties relative to the navigation of the Scheldt, and the repeal of the decree of the 19th November;—next, compenfation for the paſt, and fecurity for the future; and laſtly, the deſtruction of that ſyſtem of government or anarchy that prevails in France: and this is now held out as neceſſary even to inſure our exiſtence as a people.

Had we continued to confine ourfelves to any of the two firſt objects, I ſhould have here thought it neceſſary, before calling your attention to the probable conſequences which would have reſulted from perſevering in that ſyſtem in which we firſt embarked, or from adopting that ſyſtem which we are now purſuing, to have ſtated to you ſome ideas concerning the origin of the war. The firſt blow ſufficiently denotes

the

the firſt act of aggreſſion; but it by no means points out who, in the ſpirit of the law of nations, is the aggreſſor. When I conſider, however, that we have now embarked for the avowed purpoſe of *ſaving ourſelves*, by deſtroying the prevalent ſyſtem in France; when I learn from that conſideration, that as ſelf-preſervation neceſſarily calls forth activity, war muſt at all events have inevitably been reſolved upon in the breaſts of thoſe who could entertain this idea; and that we ſhould of courſe have been now in the ſame ſituation whatever line of conduct France had purſued, unleſs ſhe had given up that ſyſtem of interior management which it is our object to deſtroy, I ſhould think I was engaging you in an irrelevant and unprofitable enquiry.

In ſtating to you the advantages that would have attended our having remained at peace, I shall be cautious to say nothing that reason does not authorize; I will not give scope to my imagination; I feel the strength of my argument too much to think it requires it; I should weaken it in my own estimation by risking the chance of raising suspicions in your minds were I to indulge it. And I cannot but feel, that it would be unfair to arraign the judgment of those who have brought on the war, by supposing that it was practicable for them to foresee the unfortunate events that have ensued, or the enormous expence into which we have been led. I will do them the justice to say, that I do not believe there exist many individuals, who, if they could have foreseen all that has happened, and viewed the prospects which we now possess, would have given way either to views of interest or feelings of alarm, to such a degree as to prevent their supporting the mo-

tion

tion of Mr. Fox on the 18th December, 1792, which might have happily fecured to the country a chance of accommodating the then fubfifting differences.

At the time we embarked in the war, we had experience of the advantages which our trade and commerce had derived from peace, and of the national profperity that had enfued from our perfeverance in it. And if the impoverifhed ftate of the people of thofe countries, who had antecedently engaged in hoftilities, had diminifhed in certain inftances the demand for our manufactures in fome of thofe markets to which they ufed to be carried, whilft it exhibited to our eyes a picture of the confequences attending war, from which we might have benefited, the eftimation in which we were held afforded a reafonable profpect of our being able, by mediation, to check the evil

if

if it became important; and by reſtoring peace to Europe, to ſtop the growth of that habit of the love of military glory and enterpriſe, which was entwined with the exiſtence of the monarchy of France, though under the new ſyſtem it had not as yet had time thoroughly to take root. If unfortunately we had not ſucceeded in immediately reſtoring general peace, we had at all events the advantage, from the neglect which had pervaded the commerce of other countries, in conſequence of the confuſion in which they were involved, of, in a manner, monopolizing the trade of Europe. If the ſale of ſome of our manufactures was likely to be reduced, it was probable that in others it would be much augmented;—the demand for the pottery of Staffordſhire might have been diminiſhed; but the looms of Yorkſhire and Lancaſhire, and the furnaces of Birmingham, were, from the ſituation

of

of Europe, sure of increased employment; and the receipts of the country, on the whole, were likely to be much extended.—If hostilities were persevered in by the other powers of Europe, we had the prospect of at least enjoying that satisfaction which would arise from seeing our riches and our resources increasing, and our debts diminishing; whilst those of our rival were lavished in unproductive expenditure, and her people losing the habits of productive labour. The nature of the warfare in which France was engaged, as it involved her in great expence, and furnished no employment for her navy, held out no ill-grounded hope of a general neglect in her marine department; and the extinction of her commerce annihilating in a degree the nursery for her seamen, taught us to flatter ourselves, that by persevering in peace we should see our only rival on the sea gradually

dually lofe the means and the habit of dif-. playing her ftrength on that element, and offered to us at once the pleafing and the proud profpect of being able to maintain the dominion of the ocean with increafed certainty and diminifhed expence.

When the hour of general peace arrived, we had, by purfuing this line, the happinefs to forefee that the increafe of our capital, the diminution of our debt, and confequently of our taxes—the habits of induftry which we muft have acquired, the improvement in machinery, which time, ingenuity, and enterprife infure, would have enabled us to maintain our commercial fuperiority, and to meet in every market in the world our old rival, even though from the diminution and equalization of her taxes, from the additional energy of her new government, and from the enjoyment

of

of liberty ever propitious to commerce, she should start with advantages the effects of which we had not heretofore experienced. —And by thus increasing our industry and opulence, by extending our commerce, we were led with certainty to anticipate its effects in raising our importance abroad, whilst, by the wealth and happiness enjoyed at home, it was equally certain fundamentally to establish the love of our constitution in the heart of every man. For " Perish our commerce, let our constitution " survive *!" involves a paradox that it would be treating your understandings with contempt to investigate.

If, in contemplating our prospects in remaining at peace, this pleasing picture presented itself to our eye; in viewing the pro-

* A sentiment advanced by authority in the House of Commons.

bable events and confequences of warfare, we faw all thofe calamities which ufually attend that fituation, and which to us, who depend fo much on our manufactures and our commerce, is more dreadful than it can be to any other nation.

We had a fure and certain profpect of the increafe of our national debt, which had been augmented during the American war to a fum that at the moment feemed to threaten us with deftruction,—to a fum which threw ridicule on the limited ideas of thofe who had antecedently fpeculated on the fubject *, and taught man to doubt whether the world was not as yet too much in its infancy to furnifh materials, on which to build our reafoning on matters of political œconomy.—We had indeed been enabled, by the increafe of opulence which we de-

* Hume's Effay on Public Credit, Note annexed to it.

rived from the induftry and ingenuity of our manufacturers, as well as from the aid and affiftance to labour, and the variety of its effects, which the ingenious application of mechanifm and chemiftry in the conduct of our manufactures had fortunately for this country produced, to difcharge during peace the intereft of our enormous debt, and even to make provifion for the reduction of it. — But all were convinced of the difadvantage under which we laboured, in having fo large a part of our wealth emp'oyed in unproductive ufes; and there were none who did not look forward with alarm, who did not dread the confequences of thus burying any larger proportion of our productive capital.

We could not but forefee the temporary diminution of our trade, from the natural tendency that war has, both abroad and at home, to diminifh the demand for our manufactures;

factures; and the disadvantage that would arise from diverting the hands and the habits of so many of our industrious manufacturers from productive to unproductive labour, could not for a moment escape our observation.

But before we became enamoured of, and ultimately resolved upon, this system, the circumstances of the times, the situation of the nation with which we were going to contest, led naturally to anticipate in the present warfare, the hour of more than usual calamity.

We saw that we were about to engage in an unequal contest. Ours was a government that, in estimating its resources, could not totally lose sight of the happiness and prosperity of the people over which it ruled. —Theirs was a government that found refources in robbery and murder, whofe means of expenditure were alone to be eftimated by the extent of the property of the nation, and the number of whofe warriors could alone be limited in our imaginations by the number of which the community confifted.

Our military experience, and that of our allies, the circumftance of almoft all thofe having retired from France who poffeffed experience in the art of war, gave us indeed a reafonable ground to expect a temporary fuccefs. But whilft reafon, general principle and experience, taught us to ridicule the idea that courage belonged peculiarly to any nation, or was exclufively the effect of any particular climate;—it was difficult to fee why fuperiority of capital, and the extended application of labour arifing from the number of hands they could command, fhould

not in war, as in other trades, enfure
fuccefs *.

When we viewed the affertion made on
plaufible and good grounds, in Sir James

* The following extr ct of a letter from the Duke
of York, publifhed in the Gazette fince this was written, feems ftrongly to confirm this opinion:

" The hazard of an action with fuch a very great
" difparity of numbers, could not but become a matter
" of the moft ferious confideration; and, after the moft
" mature deliberation, I did not think myfelf at liberty
" to rifk, in fo unequal a conteft, his Majefty's troops,
" or thofe of his allies ferving with them. I had the
" utmoft reliance on their courage and difcipline, and I
" had no doubt but that thefe would have enabled me to
" refift the firft efforts of the enemy; but it could
" fcarcely be expected that even by the utmoft exertion
" of thefe qualities they would be able to withftand the
" reiterated attacks, which the vaft fuperiority of the
" enemy would enable them to make, and which we
" know, from experience, is a general principle upon
" which they act."

Stuart's

Stuart's Political Œconomy, how much reaſon had we to be alarmed!

"Were any prince in Europe, whoſe ſub-
"jects I ſhall ſuppoſe may amount to ſix
"millions of inhabitants, one half employed
"in agriculture, the other half employed
"in trade and induſtry, or living upon a
"revenue already acquired; were ſuch a
"prince, I ſay, ſuppoſed to have autho-
"rity ſufficient to engage his people to
"adopt a new plan of œconomy, calculated
"to ſecure them againſt the deſigns of a pow-
"erful neighbour, who, I ſhall ſuppoſe, has
"formed ſchemes of invading and ſubduing
"them: let him engage the whole proprie-
"tors of lands to renounce their ſeveral poſſeſ-
"ſions; or, if that ſuppoſition ſhould ap-
"pear too abſurd, let him contract debts to
"the value of the whole property of the
"nation; let the land tax be impoſed at
"twenty ſhillings in the pound, and then
"let

" let him become bankrupt to his creditors.
" —Let the income of all the lands be col-
" lected throughout the country for the use
" of the State; let all the luxurious arts be
" proscribed; and let those employed in them
" be formed, under the command of the for-
" mer land proprietors, into a body of regu-
" lar troops, officers and soldiers, provided
" with every thing necessary for their main-
" tenance, and that of their wives and fami-
" lies, at the public expence. Let me carry
" the supposition further. Let every su-
" perfluity be cut off; let the peasants be
" enslaved, and obliged to labour the ground
" with no view of profit to themselves, but
" for simple subsistence; let the use of gold
" and silver be proscribed, and let all these
" metals be shut up in a public treasure.
" Let no foreign trade, and very little do-
" mestic, be encouraged; but let every
" man willing to serve as a soldier be re-
" ceived and taken care of; and those who
                                    " either

" either incline to be idle, or who are found
" superfluous, be sent out of the country.
" I ask what combination, among the mo-
" dern European princes, would carry on a
" successful war against such a people ? What
" article would be wanting to their ease,
" that is, to their ample subsistence ?"

We could not but reflect that we were about to engage with a nation more emphatically in the situation he describes, than it was possible for man antecedently to imagine could have existed;—with a nation where the only difference seemed to be, that it consisted on the lowest calculation of twenty-five millions of inhabitants, and enjoyed a degree of opulence proportionate to its extended territory.

The proposal made by France, to give to maritime commerce the same protection which the law of nations secures to private property

property by land *, had been by us treated with contempt; but we could not now be blind to the situation of our commerce, and of theirs; to the little opportunity which presented itself to us of injuring them, to the extensive damages which from them in our situation we might sustain. It could not escape us, that our interference would naturally draw their attention to their marine; and we had then, as we have now, just reason to dread the consequences that their unlimited exertions, both in expence and labour, added to their superior skill in shipbuilding, would enable them to make.

* See Note presented by Chauvelin to Lord Grenville, dated 25th July 1792.

" In conformity to the express orders of his Court,
" the undersigned Minister Plenipotentiary of the King
" of the French has the honour to transmit a copy of
" a ministerial dispatch of the 13th of June, relative
" to measures to be taken by the Maritime Powers for
" the abolition of privateering."

At

At the commencement of the American war, the probability of the conteſt had been long foreſeen; the trade of our merchants was more limited;—they had time to arrange their affairs, and their ſituation enabled them to do it with eaſe:—but here the change of ſyſtem was about to be ſo ſudden, the trade of the country was ſo great, the paper credit ſo extended, that we could not but anticipate the ſhock we were likely to give to our commerce, the riſque we ran of giving a vital blow to the commercial credit of our country.

Whilſt theſe calamities naturally preſented themſelves to the mind of the man who reaſoned upon the ſubject, it was impoſſible to extract from the imaginations of thoſe whoſe ſanguine folly had made them conceited about their views of ideal ſucceſs, a prophecy of any event which reaſonably afforded proſpects of advantage, or even of indemnity

indemnity for the sure loss we were to sustain.

When we were told that their settlements in the East, their colonies in the West, would fall an easy prey, it readily occurred to *our minds*, that though the acquisition in the East Indies might have appeared formerly of great use, insomuch as it would have disabled France from carrying on those intrigues amongst the native powers which had so often disturbed the peace of India, and involved us in war,—that now, when she had withdrawn in a degree her attention from that quarter, and was completely engrossed by the war on the Continent, and her situation at home, it could alone be estimated by the value and extent of the territory we acquired,—and that in this view it could form but a trifling article on the creditor side of the account. And whilst the extent of the advantages attending the

acquisition

acquisition of the West Indies presents to the mind, if they could be retained, a very difficult object of political enquiry, estimated even by the most sanguine, it could appear but a poor compensation for the calamities that might ensue.

When we were told, with a degree of folly which was well described as throwing ridicule on the attempt of Cervantes to paint a disordered imagination *, that the exertions of the force we were likely to combine against her would ensure the conquest of France, even that was a thing which we could not seriously contemplate without alarm; for, whichever plan we looked at as likely to be pursued in consequence of it, the prospect seemed equally gloomy; we could not help foreseeing more of calamity than chance of indemnification, whether we anticipated the destruction of the balance

* See Mr. Fox's Letter to the Electors of Westminster.

of power in Europe by the partition of France, or the neceffity of maintaining the authority of any government which by force we might eftablifh over it.

Poffeffed of a form of government which we all loved and admired, it was with juft dread and alarm that we faw the progrefs of the practice of the government of one country interfering by force in the interior arrangements of another: the conduct of the Northern Powers with regard to Poland had with juftice difgufted the nation;—and as the doctrine made ftrides, as the fcenes of its exertion approached nearer to us, if the prudence of our interfering to put an end to it could be doubted by any, the folly of our giving it fanction by adopting it ourfelves was apparent to all; it was to check the principle of the right of interference that we were alone interefted, and it fignified not to us, whether the attempt was made on the

part

part of the preponderant members of the Germanic body, to deluge France with blood in endeavouring to restore the authority of its monarch against his own and his people's inclination;—or on the part of the Jacobins to affiliate the people of Bruffels with the sword, and attempt by force what they called the emancipation of mankind. The spirit of our happy Constitution was fortunately as little congenial to the principles of the one, as of the other; and it mattered not to us which of the political crusaders succeeded in their enterprise. For we could not forget, that if the Jacobins, when they talked of the monarchical part of our government, insulted our ears by ridiculing what they impiously termed a *tigre couronné*;—the conspirators of Pilnitz listened with joy to the ridicule of any share of power being possessed by what, with equal impiety, was termed *The Representatives of the Swinish Multitude*.

To

To interfere with our mediation might have prevented the melancholy extent of the evil;—to interfere as a party unavoidably tended to increase it. If after every attempt to negotiate, to avoid by every peaceable exertion the calamity, we had been reduced to the unfortunate necessity of engaging, reason would have taught us to regret the disaster: but to plunge headlong into the calamity, without taking advantage of the various opportunities that presented themselves of avoiding it;—without endeavouring anxiously to wave all the little formalities and punctilios that might stand in our way in the course of attempting by treaty to shun it, is a line which crooked policy or passion may have led us to adopt, which reason never could have permitted us to approve.

Such is the view of the subject that suggested

gested doubts of the prudence of the system at its commencement, that has led me to maintain those doubts during its progress, and that now makes me look back with regret at every opportunity of endeavouring, by negotiation, to secure or restore the peace of Europe, which we have neglected—that makes me regret, that when in July 1792 France solicited our mediation, and our allies hardly could have refused it, we thought proper not to interfere, on account of the formality of all the parties concerned not having applied to us, and the aversion we then so strongly expressed to taking a part in the internal affairs of another country*—that makes me lament, that in Au-

* It is not easy to understand how our interference for the purpose of mediation, the thing M. Chauvelin solicited, could be stated by Lord Grenville to be inconsistent with the rights and the independence of the allies.—See Lord Grenville's Letter to M. Chauvelin, Whitehall, July 8, 1792.

guft 1792 we thought it neceffary to recall our Minifter from Paris:—a ftep which, if we look at the conduct of the European Powers in the revolution in the Netherlands—during the Commonwealth or at the revolution in England—during all the various revolutions in the Conftitutions of Denmark, Sweden, Bohemia, and Hungary, the practice of former times feems not to vindicate, and to which our own conduct in the recent revolutions of Poland and Flanders gives no countenance:—a ftep, the prudence of which it will be difficult to defend, when we confider that there never was a time in which we fhould fo anxioufly have wifhed for information of the interior fituation of France; or in which, upon an enlarged view of our interefts, it feemed fo defirable for us, by well-judged interpofition, amicably to put an end to the war in which fhe was engaged.

But

But above all I must sincerely regret, that in December 1792, when every sort of security was offered to Holland; when an explanation of the decree of the 19th December was given, which it will be difficult for those who have since united Corsica to the Crown of England to arraign; when opening the navigation of the Scheldt seemed the only point in dispute—that we did not adopt the motion of Mr. Fox, as a prelude to a negotiation; and that we should have considered the punctilio, whether we should treat with an acknowledged Minister or secret Agent, to be of importance sufficient for us to sacrifice to it all chance of amicable arrangement.

It is this view of the subject, coupled with a sense of the calamities we have suffered, and the situation in which we now stand, that creates in my mind much sorrow that we treated with contempt the offer made us in April 1793 *, as well as another propofal which was fubfequently made in the autumn of the fame year;—that we did not avail ourfelves of the means which the expulfion of the French from Flanders, and the defertion of Dumourier in May 1793, gave us of propofing terms to them;—or of that opportunity we fince poffeffed from our temporary advantages on the Continent, and our fucceffes in the Weft Indies, of

* See Le Brun's Letters, dated April 2, 1793, communicated to Lord Grenville through Mr. Salter, Notary Public.

Though the commencing a treaty through the medium of a Notary is undoubtedly novel, we ought to confider that it was difficult at the time to devife a mode of communication.—And a knowledge of French habits teaches us, that they naturally annex to this mode of proceeding much more ferious formality than it conveys to an Englifh ear.—When the Parliament of Paris were refufed accefs to the King, we find them taking a proteft before a Notary.

offering

offering what to them muſt in reaſon have appeared advantageous terms.

Were I diſpoſed to flatter myſelf, that in reviewing all thoſe ſcenes, that in peruſing what I have ſtated to you in defence of the meaſures I have uniformly ſupported, you may have found any thing which has induced you to heſitate, or doubt whether they may not be founded in truth; and whether, if that line of conduct had been adopted to which they would have naturally led, it might not have tended to the preſervation of peace, and the conſequent increaſe of our internal opulence and external importance.—I am however well aware, that before I can have any well-founded hopes of vindicating my conduct in your eſtimation, there is another mode in which the ſubject has been argued, and in which it is neceſſary for me to conſider it.

I have not forgot the cant of the advocate for war. I know on what he has harped. I recollect that the prophecy of destruction to the Constitution in the event of peace, is the spell with which he has enchanted the minds of those who have listened to him; that the annihilation of property, and the existence in this country of all those scenes of blood which we beheld with horror, is the dreadful threat with which he has subdued the minds, and for a moment arrested the reasoning faculties, of the community. It was well, it was artfully chosen. In a country, among the inhabitants of which property was more generally and universally diffused than in any other; where there exist few whose industry has not put them in possession of something which they find an interest in preserving;—in a country, the spirit of whose criminal laws and political institutions had

universally

universally infused in the minds of its inhabitants a mild spirit of benevolence—it was with certainty you might predict its effect; it was sure to rouse the feelings, to influence the passions of the people; and when properly wound up, it required no great art and eloquence to guide the mind of the nation, to turn the fury of the moment against France, which the people of this country had long been accustomed to consider as a rival, whose inhabitants they had long regarded as their natural enemies:—a feeling in a degree suspended, whilst in forming a limited monarchy *she* seemed to pay a just tribute to the wisdom of our Constitution, but which now returned with increased vigour from a sense of her impertinence, in endeavouring, in her own idea, to lead the way in political improvement, when our prejudices had long confined her talents, and limited her sway, to improvement in the shape of a gown, or in the formation of a cap.

But, indeed, it was only at the moment we were under the guidance of passion that this belief of danger to our Constitution could spread, that this doctrine of dread of a similar revolution could make its proselytes: so soon as reason presided in the mind, the idea of danger was sure to vanish. In the situation of the two countries there was not the smallest similarity. In this country, justice was administered by known rules, and by judges skilled in the laws, who held their situation for life; in that, it had been a matter of favour and solicitation, which was dealt out according to the whim or caprice of those who had purchased the privilege *. The people of this

---

* The administration of justice was partial, venal, infamous. I have, in conversation with many very
sensible

country had their reprefentatives, who, though it is anxioufly to be wifhed that they were more emphatically the reprefentatives of the people, are even now an important body of men, through whom they can ftate their grievances. In that country, the people faw no body of men who had not an intereft to conceal and augment the hardfhips under which they laboured, and who were not in the daily practice of con-

fenfible men, in different parts of the kingdom, met with fomething of content with their government, in all other refpects than this: but upon the queftion of expecting juftice to be really and fairly adminiftered, every one confeffed there was no fuch thing to be looked for. The conduct of the Parliaments was profligate and atrocious. Upon almoft every caufe that came before them, intereft was openly made with the judges; and woe betided the man who, in a caufe to fupport, had no means of conciliating favour, either by the beauty of a handfome wife, or by other methods!—A. YOUNG.

tributing

tributing towards their extent. Here there exists a nobility, intermingling with the other orders, by habit and ties of blood every where connected with the community, to whose title political power is invariably attached, who, if they had not the inclination, would, in the pursuit of their own interests, in the maintaining of their political influence, of necessity become habituated to favour and protect those beneath them. There, there existed a body of nobility isolated from the rest of the state, whose title had no political power connected with it, whose existence only served by their example to discourage industry, and whose privilege alone consisted in the power to oppress*. Though we laboured under the

---

* Besides the oppression that originated from the extent and inequality of public taxes, the exactions of the Seigneur were enormous. " What," says Mr. Young, " are these tortures of the peasantry in Bre-
" tagne,

pressure of a large debt, we levied without any conspicuous oppression a revenue equal to the discharge of the interest, and to a considerable annual diminution of the capital. In France, as the national debt increased, in consequence of the privileges and exemptions of the clergy and nobility, the taxes on the people became oppressive in a degree beyond which government dreaded to carry it*; and,

by

" tagne, which they call chevanchés; quintains;
" foul; faut de poison; baiser de mariées; transporte
" d'œuf sur un charette; silence des grenouilles; corvée
" à miséricorde; melods; leide; couponage; cartelage;
" barage; fouage; marechauffée; ban vin; ban d'août;
" trouffes; gelinage; civerage; taillabifité; vingtain;
" sterlage; bordelage; minage; ban de vendanges;
" droit d'accepte!"

* Instances, and even gross ones, have been reported to me in many parts of the kingdom, that made me shudder at the oppression to which numbers must have been condemned, by the undue favours granted to

such

by putting off the evil hour, they at laſt found the deficiency amount to the enormous ſum of upwards of three millions ſterling.— There, in the moment of ſuffering from this

ſuch crooked influence. But, without recurring to ſuch caſes, what muſt have been the ſtate of the poor people paying heavy taxes, from which the Nobility and Clergy were exempted? A cruel aggravation of their miſery, to ſee thoſe who could beſt afford to pay exempted, becauſe able! —The inrollments for the militia, which the Cahiers call injuſtice without example, were another dreadful ſcourge on the peaſantry; and, as married men were exempted from it, occaſioned in ſome degree that miſchievous population, which brought beings into the world in order for little elſe than to be ſtarved. The Corvées, or police of the roads, were annually the ruin of many hundreds of farmers; more than 300 were reduced to beggary, in filling up one vale in Lorain: all theſe oppreſſions fell on the Tiers Etat only; the Nobility and Clergy having been equally exempted from tailles, militia, and corvées. The penal code of finance makes one ſhudder at the horrors of puniſhment inadequate to the crime.—A. YOUNG.

oppreſſion,

oppreſſion, and in this deſperate ſtate of public credit, the people had been inſulted by the profuſion of the Court; they had ſeen in a few years, beſides the debts he contracted, a million ſterling, excluſive of his annual income, laviſhed by a Prince of the blood *. Here, the wiſe regulation of our laws permitted no ſuch improvident expenditure in the miniſters.

Our government was the active theme of praiſe in the mouths of every one;—theirs died a natural death, without exciting the lamentations of any:—in France, it might with truth be ſaid, that the neceſſity of a change had brought about the revolution;— in this country, it was equally true, that the

* In the Red Book produced to the Aſſemblée Conſtituante, the Count D'Artois appears to have received that ſum during the adminiſtration of M. de Calonne.

wanton

wanton love of change could alone generate the idea of one.

There, the great body of the people were more fubjected to oppreffion than in any other nation of Europe;—here undoubtedly lefs fo; and we could not forget that—"*Pour* "*la populace, ce n'eft jamais par envie d'at-* "*taquer qu'elle fe fouleve, mais par impati-* "*ence de fouffrir* *," is the fentiment of a great man and a Minifter of State; that it is the confeffion of a zealous affertor of monarchy.

Paffion and prejudice are the moft formidable enemies to the juft decifion of all queftions fubmitted to the underftanding; and though unfortunately they have often triumphed, perhaps in no inftance was their

* Sully's Memoirs.

triumph ever more conspicuous, or the dominion which in consequence of it they exclusively established over the mind of man, more complete.

Had reason been allowed to retain the smallest sway, it might perhaps have occurred, when things were going on quietly, and a new government apparently established in France, which promised to its inhabitants more felicity than they had heretofore enjoyed, that there might have existed amongst us some wrong-headed individuals, animated with a desire of imitation:—but we should have seen, in the horrors which ensued in its progress, that which was sure to command the aversion of all. In this moment of delusion, however, when passion presided exclusively in our minds, the apprehension of the desire of imitation increased as the scene became disgusting;—and when armed with

its

its antidote, the progress of the disorder became in our imaginations most likely to be alarming.

But if there was no reasonable ground on which a revolution in this country ought to have been dreaded; if it appears that in our imaginations the tendency towards it strangely seemed the most alarming, at the moment when in reality it must have been the least so; the mode of preventing it, adopted and universally relished, when examined, is that which must appear still more unaccountable.

War was the receipt held out to us to prevent all tendency to sedition, to annihilate in this country all idea of a revolution. In former times, wise men have told us, that the surest way to prevent seditions was to take away the matter of them.—
But

But our statesmen strangely saw the best preventative in that which was sure in its progress to create the matter of them. The hardships and burthens of war have in all ages tended to give rise to discontent; the expence naturally creates poverty; and Lord Bacon wisely states, that the matter of sedition is of two kinds, poverty and discontentment. It was strange then to see that the favourite means adopted to prevent a revolution, was what the experience of man had taught him to believe almost universally generated it. Nothing but the prejudice of the moment could have made it palatable; at any other time the public would have said to the rash political empiric who prescribed it, as the Cynic did of old to a friend officiously advising him to send for a physician—"If I die, I'll die at leisure."

If before entering into hostilities we had reason to dread the calamities that were likely to ensue from the war—if in it we saw not what was to prevent, but that which was much more likely to create the seditious disposition we apprehended, and the idea of revolution at which we trembled—we have received little consolation from the unfortunate events which have attended its progress. The accuracy of the predictions of those who opposed it might give rise to a little sensation of vanity, did not the melancholy situation of the country and our gloomy prospects preclude the possibility of any feeling of the kind. In the short period of eighteen months, during which we have been amused with the vague chimeras of our ministers, we have seen successively vanish before our eyes all those various sources of success with which we had vainly flattered ourselves.—Disgraced by by the impotent efforts at Toulon; banished from the northern frontier; the rebellion crushed in La Vendée—France exhibits herself more powerful than before the contest. The practice of war has taught her armies the necessity of discipline, which did not at first exist, and upon the possession of which we founded our hopes. We have seen that the want of salt-petre could by exertion be supplied. We have learnt the impossibility of starving a nation. We know that a union of foreign force against them has furnished them a common cause in which with enthusiasm they unite — perhaps, on reflection, we may have reason to apprehend, with the only thing which could have stifled their internal feuds.—We have seen the heads of their political leaders and of their generals alternately brought to the block, without any diminution of their energy: and we

have

have at laſt learned, that which we at firſt ought to have known—that the revolution of France is a revolution of opinion; that the war we are conducting is not againſt armies, but an armed nation.

We have given to a people who did not ſeem antecedently to poſſeſs it, the habit and taſte for military enterpriſe; we have taught them that, of which from experience three years ago they were as ignorant as ourſelves, that they are capable of ſucceſsfully conducting it; and unfortunately we have at once diſcloſed to them, and to the world, the ſad ſecret of their ſtrength, and of our own weakneſs. The allied armies have, during this campaign, loſt 150,000 men; and at the end of it, we ſhall in all have expended ſince the commencement of the war a ſum that cannot be reaſonably computed at leſs than thirty millions;

millions; and with all this waste of blood and treasure, if the object be the annihilation of the system in France, we have not purchased a single thing which the ingenuity of man can state as in the smallest degree tending towards our success in attaining it. Yet impetuous zeal still pervades our councils, and no one has yet asked,

"Are not the lives of those who draw the sword
"In Rome's defence, intrusted to your care?
"Should we thus lead them to a field of slaughter,
"Might not th' impartial world with reason say,
"We lavish'd at our deaths the blood of thousands
"To grace our fall, and make our ruin glorious?"

By our perseverance in hostilities we have nearly brought ourselves into the contemptible but lamentable state of a nation emphatically described by Demosthenes as being—" the terror of its allies, the laughing-"stock of its enemies." The Dutch, if they

they confider their fituation, will, as applied to us, fympathife with the firft part of the character; and the infertion of the word *dupe* is perhaps the only alteration, if he held my pen, that the King of Pruffia would be inclined to make.

It is a melancholy thing to look back and view the proud eminence from which, by adopting this fyftem, we have fallen; and ftill more fo to contemplate that height which by perfevering in an oppofite conduct we might have attained:—the very intereft of the money which we have thus lavifhly expended, added to our finking fund would have brought us at once to that enviable ftate of financial profperity, to which the minifter fanguinely announced we might have arrived in the year 1808: and it is difficult to define the limits of the degree of opulence to which that doctrine concerning the accumulation

mulation of capital (that has been ignorantly stated to have originated with Dr. Smith) would lead you in speculation to think you might arrive; or to the degree of commercial prosperity which, in consequence of the growing command of capital, we might have attained. But the most melancholy part of the picture is seen, when we view the importance which our riches, and the idea of our naval strength, had we remained neutral, would have given us in the eyes of the other nations of Europe, when contrasted with the exhausted situation in which the war must have involved them. Yet all these blessings were within our reach. Had we persevered in the system with which we started, they might in all human probability have been attained; had we, instead of conceiving the revolution in France to be a ground for involving us in war, learnt the only lesson which reason and prudence could have taught us to derive from it, they might have been secured; and by adopting a moderate and prudent reform, in the moment of peace and prosperity, of those imperfections to which every human institution is liable, they might have been perpetuated. For, notwithstanding the present unpopularity that attends the idea of reform, I am not afraid to subscribe to the doctrine of one of our greatest statesmen and philosophers, —" And if time of course alter things to the " worse, and if wisdom and counsel shall " not alter them to the better, what shall be " the end?—it were good therefore that " men in their innovations would follow " the example of time itself, which indeed " enervates greatly but quietly, and by de- " grees scarce to be perceived."—Nor can I refrain from reprobating the presumptuous folly of those who wish to restrain the reason and exertions of man from improvement

in

in government, the excellence of which forms the fureſt ſource of his happineſs and proſperity, at a time when they daily and hourly ſee the advantages derived in the more trivial concerns of life from the well conſidered application of his ingenuity.

I know there are many who pretend ſuch a reverence of this our conſtitution, as to affect to ſee even in its little imperfections freſh ſources for their daily admiration: but were I to be called upon to judge on the comparative reality of the patriotiſm of thoſe who wiſh moderate and gradual reform, and of thoſe who wiſh to preſerve the impurities with which time has impregnated our conſtitution; of thoſe who in reforming are ever watchful, " that it ſhould " be the reformation that draweth on the " change, and not the deſire of change that " pretendeth the reform,"—and of thoſe who

tremble

tremble at the idea of purging the state of any of its impurities;—reminding them of the speech of Alexander to his friends—"He-"phæstion is the friend of Alexander; Cra-"terus is the friend of the king,"—I would pronounce without fear of my judgment being impeached—You, the moderate reformer, are the real friend to the constitution. You, the obstinate admirer even of its abuses, are the friend of that which you think has brought you into power, and that which you look to as likely to preserve you in it.—Nay, were I disposed to go further, to such a man I would say, Your praise of the constitution is what I value not; it passeth away, and leaves no impression behind; I have lived too long, I have attended too constantly to the mode in which the politics of this country have been conducted, not to have learnt, that as history teaches me to regret the glory of God has since the commencement of the

world

world been too often impiously used as a prelude to the temporal interests of the clergy — so a vague and empty rhapsody upon the beauties of our glorious constitution has uniformly preceded even the most corrupt plans that any minister in pursuit of his own interest ever dared to bring forward.

Having now stated to you what I conceive to be the melancholy result of having adopted the system on which we have acted, and what would have been the fortunate consequence of our having persevered in the opposite line; thinking myself that the reason of man cannot vindicate the preference which has been given, I will endeavour to state to you in my next the circumstances from whence it has originated.

Habituated to the confideration of the public

public conduct of the different parties that exift in this country; poffeffing frequent opportunities of knowing the private fprings that have actuated them; it will in my next letter be my endeavour to trace the fyftem to its legitimate parent, to fhew you how it was generated by the art of fome and the folly of others; how it owes its origin folely to intrigues for power in the interior of this country.

LETTER

LETTER II.

Southend, Essex, Sept. 20th, 1794.

IT has hitherto been my principal view to endeavour to point out to you that the real interests of this country, impartially considered and well understood, would have led us to persevere in our original system of neutrality. That there was no absolute state necessity for our departure from it, appears sufficiently obvious. That reason never could have dictated a dereliction of its beneficial and salutary principles, is equally clear. And when I reflect on the chance of calamity which even Ministers themselves must have anticipated, from the measures they were resolved to adopt, I am forced to look for some other cause that must have guided them in their operations, than any of those ostensible reasons and feeble pleas they have hitherto held out to the Parliament and the public.

Nor does this inveſtigation ſeem to be a taſk of much difficulty: their actuating principle is eaſily defined; though to ſtate it with the hopes of conviction, when the public mind has been ſo long warped by erroneous opinions, is hardly poſſible.

Accuſtomed as almoſt all have been to view the preſent ſituation of the country as the reſult of one particular cauſe, however much it may be founded in original error, it muſt be difficult to eradicate the prejudice. Habitual indulgence muſt naturally have added to its ſtrength; nor could it eaſily be ſuppoſed, when the feelings of the moment had connected in the minds of almoſt all, the ſalvation of every thing that is dear to us with engaging in hoſtilities, that

the

the language of peace could be the language of popularity; or that the dictates of reason could soon gain an ascendancy over prejudice so inveterate, and delusion so complete. I could not therefore but be sensible of the difficulties attending my undertaking; and the anxiety this feeling naturally gave, the diffidence which it unavoidably created, may possibly have induced me to dwell more at length than perhaps I needed to have done (in this moment of calamity), in proving to you, that the war never could have originated from any just hopes of promoting the welfare of this country. It is that feeling also which now leads me, with a view to strengthen any impression I may have made upon you, to go further, and shew from what it actually did take its rise. The man accused, who produces in court the real criminal, exhibits the strongest and most conclusive proof of his own innocence.

I shall

I shall not however here confine myself fingly to that object. Deep as the calamity is, which this country has suffered by being plunged into war, the measures of ministers have produced evils of a different, though of a very serious nature. By their arts we have seen broken down, and in a manner annihilated, the importance of a party which had long distinguished itself for its temperate and steady adherence to the real interests of the people. An eager and uniform supporter of that party, since I first engaged in politics; distinguished alone for my attachment to it when elected your representative; I had not presumption enough to look on your preference of me in any other light than as a mark of your predilection for it. To you therefore I cannot conceive that an account of the circumstances which have brought it into its present situation can be uninteresting. To me it is necessary; for,

for, if I hope to retain your approbation, it is requisite to shew I had no share in demolishing the party, by giving a feeble support to which I am conscious I first acquired my only title to the possession of your favour.

The topics too are so much interwoven —the origin of the war, and the state into which that party is now brought, are subjects so much connected—that to treat of the one without touching upon the other would be impossible; to treat of them separately difficult.

Long convinced that the welfare of this country depends upon the existence of a body connected on those principles the Whig party has been understood to possess; that the nature of its government creates it; that its preservation demands it; I am by

principle

principle a party-man; and it is therefore with pleasure I take the opportunity that this connection with the origin of the war gives me, of stating to you the utility of such combination under the government of this country, and of tracing shortly the history of that party whose fate I have now to lament, so far as is necessary to explain the situation of those personally concerned in politics at the beginning of the revolution in France.—I shall then be led to point out to you the origin and progress of the intrigue that had for its object to secure the possession of power, which has unfortunately deprived the nation of the advantage derived from so great a body of men united in the cause of freedom, and drawn upon it all the numerous misfortunes with which this war is likely to be attended.

By

By exhibiting the advantages which in this country we derive from a united body of men acting on principle, I hope to convince you, that though the calamities of war (the involving us in which was the facrifice Mr. Pitt made to the Duke of Portland and his friends) are more immediately felt; their ultimate confequences cannot prove more ferioufly deplorable than the breaking up of the Whig party—the facrifice that he gradually contrived they fhould make to him.

In endeavouring to eftablifh the advantages of the exiftence of party in this country, I know I am about to lay down and defend a doctrine againft which there exifts a prejudice fo general, that whilft we fee in times paft there is hardly any misfortune the hiftorian does not rack his genius to trace home to this caufe, fo we now uniformly hear all the misfortunes and calamities of the day vaguely attributed to the

exertions

exertions of party-spirit, and the existence of party-feeling.

But a very little reflection must enable any one to detect the fallacy of the idea, and teach him to reject the opinion, with respect to this country, however generally it may be received.

Party in reality will be found to be attended with advantage, just in proportion to the degree the government under which it exists admits of its being founded on principle: in the simple forms of government there is no possible difference in principle which can give rise to combination; and therefore party under them must always be productive of temporary, often of permanent evil.

In a monarchy or a republic there can be no parties arising from difference in principle

principle but such as give birth to confusion; they afford no subjects on which to combine, but such as from their nature must tend to generate immediate convulsion. In the one, a difference of opinion with regard to the right to the crown, or a desire totally to overturn the government, upon account of real or ideal oppression, both possessing the seeds of instant conflict, are the only topics for which our imaginations enable us to conceive men can wish to combine, or that the annals of times past shew us they have united. There are under such a government no jarring principles upon which you can maintain different opinions; the possession of power depends solely on the favour of the Sovereign, and favour is always more easily secured by individual address than by combined effort. In the other, the object which parties must naturally have, and which history points out as their main pursuit, is merely to support the pretensions of different individuals to public favour; and whilst we recollect the evils of the disturbances attending such contests, we cannot but remember how often they have ended solely, in being the means of advancing the man of brilliant talents in preference to him whose more sound pretensions were founded upon the purity of his intentions;—how often the crafty has been able to make party the engine of his elevation, at the expence of the able, the virtuous and discerning statesman.

In aristocracies, the object of parties has been to support the pretensions of different families to power; and though we have always seen them produce immediate calamity, it is in vain we look for any permanent benefit to the society, to compensate for the momentary evil. The struggle is here alone for who shall have the privilege of oppression; and the conduct of all men in power,

power, if not well watched, has but too great a refemblance to make us think that fuch a conteſt can produce any laſting good.

In our conſtitution, however, of which in theory we are taught to admire the beauties, as proceeding from a due mixture of the different forms of government, there muſt arife naturally a difference of opinion on principle. He who gives himſelf up to the purſuit of honours and dignities, who loves the ſplendour of a court, attaches himſelf to the cauſe of monarchy, and foon fees in the increaſed power of the monarch the fource of additional weight and ſplendour to thoſe who furround the throne, and of increaſing value to the favours which the fovereign can confer. He who poſſeſſes an ardent mind, conſcious of its own rectitude, animated with a defire of building reputation upon a more folid foundation, naturally looks with anxious defire to acquire the approbation and applause of his fellow citizens, and discovers with equal alacrity, in the extent of the power which they may possess or retain, the value of that he wishes to obtain.

Such a difference of opinion cannot long subsist without the existence of party founded on principle. The friends of monarchy have in the person of the monarch a common bond of union; they derive from his councils a source of unity of action.

Poor and feeble would be the resistance which the isolated efforts of the disunited advocates of freedom could make against such an attack; there is nothing in their pursuit which naturally connects them. But they must soon see the necessity of uniting to preserve the value of that for which they all contend against the efforts of those who, from their situation, naturally present themselves in phalanx.—The folly of resisting

the

the attack of an invading enemy by individual exertion, is too great, too apparent not soon to generate, under such a government as ours, the appearance of popular party to counteract the effects of court intrigue. And as in the form of our constitution we perceive a natural tendency to produce a party of this description, so the benefits that must arise from it are too obvious not to strike any man who suffers his mind to consider the subject. Under the simple forms of government, party can alone tend to overturn the existing constitution, or to create temporary disturbances, without affording the hopes of permanent benefit. Under our mixed form of government, party on principle has a direct propensity effectually to preserve a due balance between the various branches of the government; and by the powerful check, which through this means the supporters of free-

dom are enabled to give to the gradual encroachments of the Crown, it has a tendency to prevent that ultimate difturbance, which the imperceptible extenfion of influence is fure to create, when it has made fuch advances that the " hoary head of in-
" veterate abufe can no longer draw reve-
" rence or obtain protection from the mul-
" titude."

If, in confidering the theory of our conftitution, we find this principle arifing out of its very nature; if we difcover, fo far from being likely to fuftain any detriment or injury from its adoption, that it always muft prove itfelf a great prop to the vigour and ftability of our government—when we defcend to view its practice, party will then appear more than ever neceffary; the benefits arifing from it will be ftill more confpicuous.

For

For if party conſtituted on ſound principle, when we conſider the conſtitution as theory repreſents it, ſeemed to form its beſt nouriſhment ;—when cramped and crippled by its habitual diſorder, corruption—it is the beſt medicine that the wiſdom of the politician can preſcribe; in proportion as corruption increaſes it becomes neceſſary; and now, when in a manner it has univerſally pervaded the frame of the government, without ſuch a combination we can hardly look with hopes of ſafety to its exiſtence.

To engage you in an inveſtigation of the gradual departure of our conſtitution in practice, from that ſtate of purity in which the theoriſt repreſents it; to ſtate to you the mode in which the government is now practically conducted; to lay open to you all the numerous channels of corruption daily practiſed to influence the minds of
the

the community; to difcover the art of forming a parliament, as it is called (which conftitutes the chief excellence of the Secretay of the Treafury); to trace the pains and trouble that is taken to learn the mode in which the fentiments and conduct of individuals, from the higheft to the loweft, can be rendered fubfervient to their views of felf-intereft (which forms a branch of the bufinefs of fome underling in every office in the kingdom); to exhibit to you the various attempts which have been made, and are daily making, to caufe this our happy conftitution filently to dwindle into a defpotifm of influence—would lead me into a wider field than is confiftent with the profecution of my prefent plan; and the underftanding of it in detail is unfortunately not neceffary to convince you, or any one who lives in this country, that the habit of corruption has more deeply and univerfally pervaded the community,

community, than it ever did any people of whofe manners and cuftoms we have a diftinct account. To difcover the caufe of this, requires not much greater exertion of our reafon, than it unfortunately does of our obfervation to perceive the effects.

Power and political importance, which have been the defire, the anxious wifh and the purfuit of the ambitious in all ages, have under different governments been acquired or obtained by various means;—by the favour of the people—by the partiality of the monarch—by private intrigue—by open canvafs—by public difplay of opulence and magnificence;—nay, even by fecret largefs. But it was referved to the *practice* of this conftitution, to exhibit to the eye political power not only fecretly obtained by indirect means, but become the

object

object of open and avowed sale and purchase; to see a market price affixed to the guardianship of the rights of the people, and the usufruct, the possession or the reversion of it, alternately brought under the hammer *.

New as this phenomenon is, its consequences are obvious. Money in a country where such abuses prevail acquires a novel and additional value, a value of the most dangerous kind, which it was never known antecedently to possess; for, as it thus supplants the necessity of exhibiting character and public spirit, which should be the sole recommendation to favour

* To state examples of the two former must be unnecessary; the fact is notorious. But it has been reserved for the refined corruption of the present times, to sell even the reversion of national representation—an instance of which I could now state.

and confidence, it establishes itself in request, just as it discourages the habit and the fashion of cultivating every thing that is virtuous, and which ought to lead to the acquiring of power. The influence of this open and corrupt traffic cannot be supposed to confine itself to the elector. The man who by his virtue has recommended himself to the favour of others, whose patriotism and ability have formed the ground of their predilection—when their representative, naturally regards a perseverance in the line of virtue and real patriotism to be the surest mode of securing a continuance of their partiality, and a renewal of that trust with which they have invested him. But the man who has acquired it by purchase, with equal justice, and in reality arguing upon the same principle, can consider it alone as useful in so far as he may make it conduce to the filling up that blank, created

created by the price he has paid, in his capital; or perhaps of increafing his ftock in trade, and by that means of enabling him to return with additional recommendation to a future canvas;—and thus, with the fame indifference for the meafures he fupports that his conftituents had for the perfon they elected, he is led at once to difplay with true fympathy in *his* fphere, the feelings that actuated them in *theirs*;—and the corruption of the reprefentative foon becomes as open and avowed as that of his conftituents.

If commerce, riches, and the luxurious habits they produce, have had at all times a natural tendency to create venality, how much ftronger muft be their effect in a climate fo propitious to the growth of corruption! The fure confequence that muft attend the increafe of wealth and luxury

under

under a government so completely impregnated with an open and avowed system of corruption, upon national character, is too obvious to require illustration. No one doubts a despotic government is calculated to render men pliant, and a free one resolute and independent; no one can doubt that excessive venality will be the characteristic of a people reared under such a government. Refinement of manners cannot be more natural to the courtier, bluntness and sincerity to the man born under a popular government, than the study of his own self-interest must be to the man so trained.

From openly pursuing it, and sacrificing every other consideration to this feeling, there can arise among such a people no shame; every one is familiarised to it from his infancy; custom has rendered it habitual; and it is soon alone

alone regarded as what is called the way of the world—something which either may or must be practised to hinder us from being the dupes of our own integrity. From the highest to the lowest it must shew itself equally the leading principle that directs the conduct of every one; and we cannot be surprised at seeing the proverbial apology of a poor domestic, when quitting his indulgent master, become familiar to all—nay, the first in rank and fortune, in endeavouring *to better themselves*, feeling an ample compensation for every dereliction of opinion and every desertion of principle.

When government has come to be thus in practice carried on, when this mode of conducting it has prevailed for such a length of time as to have had its full effect in moulding the character and forming the sentiments of the community, party on principle becomes more than ever neceſſary; individual effort is not only inefficacious, but it is almoſt impoſſible that it ſhould exiſt in any great extent. To expect from any man, that the pure ſenſe of virtue and patriotiſm ſhould enable him to conquer in himſelf all thoſe deſires and habits with which the ſyſtem of his education, precept, example, and the manners of the ſociety have ſtamped his character, and that he ſhould exhibit perſeverance in this conduct when he ſees that it commands the applauſe of none, is almoſt impoſſible. But it is wild and romantic to think, that there can be many ſuch inſtances of individual forbearance, when we reflect that the general venality which is thus produced has rendered the ſacrifice of public principle (if the price is approved), whatever rank, age, or ſex, you look to, ſure of commanding the ſympathy of all, the approbation and applauſe of moſt.—The man whoſe feelings, from early impreſſion, have been from infancy in uniſon with the ſentiments which this political depravity has generated; or he who, in paſſing from the college to the commerce of the world, has in compliance with conſtant cuſtom ſacrificed ſooner or later to the ruling propenſities of the ſociety every principle to which his mind was attached, are equally ready to mark with admiration the conduct of ſuch a proſelyte;—and even the woman, who, in compliment to the morality of the times, has made the early but important ſacrifice of affection to intereſt, and now in affluence leads a comfortable life, remote from the man to whom the ſympathies of her mind attached her, flattered with authority that ſeems to countenance and ſanction her conduct, is ready to join in the general chorus of applauſe.

In ſuch a ſituation, to reſiſt the progreſſive

five annihilation of every thing like patriotism, even with the affiftance to be derived from the combined effort of party, is difficult; without it, impoffible. Through the medium however of party formed on principle, we obvioufly acquire the means of giving to the little remnant of public virtue that is to be found, all the vigour which it can derive from the affiftance of private fentiments of honour in the breafts of thofe who are in any degree connected with it. Friendfhip, relationfhip, all the ties which are capable of connecting or attaching men, become by this means fucceffively auxiliaries in the caufe of public virtue, and unite their ftrength to enable it to make its laft ftand againft the efforts of overgrown corruption; nay, even venality itfelf is often forced for the moment into the fervice of virtue, and men with benefit to the community are taught to ftem their natural propenfity to give way to

immediate

immediate corruption, whilſt they glut themſelves with the views of future benefits which their imagination preſents to them.

To ſuppoſe that even party (however ſkilfully conducted) in ſuch a conteſt can be ſuccefsful, is difficult; but all muſt agree that it arms the minds of thoſe attached to it with the moſt powerful weapon to reſiſt the vicious propenſities created by the mode of conducting our government; and that it enables us to erect the only fortreſs in defence of public virtue, even the outworks of which have for a ſeries of years ſhewn themſelves impregnable when aſſailed by corruption.

But the good effects of party in the preſent ſituation of this country reſt not even here. Thoſe who are thus by various means united, get individually pledged to a ſyſtem

system of conduct; and if they afterwards attain power, private honour becomes (greatly to the advantage of the public) a spur to the recollection of the minister, who from the corruption incident to the situation is but too apt to forget every principle he antecedently possessed.

Party too naturally draws the attention of all. The community at large, some from principle, most from views of immediate or remote interest, become the adherents of those in possession of power, or of those connected on principle: their disputes attract and monopolize the attention of the community, and thus effectually protect our constitution from the licentious investigation of the ignorant, the busy and aspiring, and give time for the hand of the skilful, uninterrupted by tumult, to administer those preventatives against the undermining effects of time, which in all human institutions are necessary, and which all wise politicians will adopt. Numerous were the elogies and lampoons on the mistresses and the ministers of the kings of France that used formerly to be handed about; infinite are the numbers of satires, essays and pamphlets, which in this country have appeared to exhibit the political depravity of ministers, or their opponents; and we cannot but observe, that whilst the wit and the talents of the community have been thus employed and exhausted, the beauties of the constitution and the virtues of the grand monarch have formed equally the theme of the vague praise of the multitude *.

The

---

* That the existence of party has thus protected the constitution; that it has thus secured to it the admiration of all, even without enquiry, by monopolizing

the

The theorist in politics may harangue against party, as the moralist has often done against that false system of honour which in modern times has given rise to duelling, and guides in a degree the intercourse of life; but as the advantage of the one is in society apparent to all, there is none who has attended to the mode in which this government is in practice conducted, who must not be convinced of the benefit and even the necessity of the other: indeed the marked aversion uniformly shewn to it by the courtier, is not a stronger proof of his sense of its salutary effect in restraining the corrupt influence of the Crown, than

the attention; none can doubt, when we reflect, that though the volumes are numerous indeed which have been written on the subject of party controversy, there exists no one work by a native of this country, which confines itself to the consideration of our constitution, and professes to treat of it at large.

the

the eager and conſtant attacks of the advocates of The Rights of Man are of their feeling of its tendency to preſerve our conſtitution.

It was theſe idea of this extreme utility of party, under the government of this country as it is conducted in practice, that muſt have led thoſe who acted on principle to unite in forming and ſupporting that party which Lord Rockingham paſſed his life in rearing, and which Mr. Fox has uniformly exerciſed his talents in maintaining and ſupporting.

Their object has at all times undoubtedly been to acquire power; for " Power to do " good is the true and lawful end of aſpir- " ing. Good thoughts towards men are little " better than good dreams, except they are " put in act; and that cannot be without " power

" power and place as the vantage and
" commanding ground *."—But they difclaimed court intrigue as the mode of acquiring it, and rejected corruption as the
fole means of retaining it: they fought
to make their courfe regular, that men
might know before hand what they had to
expect; and looked to that attachment which
the principles they poffeffed ought to have
created in the minds of the people, to that refpect which they muft have commanded in
the breaft of the fovereign, as the only channel through which they could attain power
with any probable benefit to the community.

If habit had rendered it impracticable to
carry on the government without corruption, their fyftem, by calling in principle to
its aid, tended at leaft gradually to diminifh
the neceffity of the extent of it.—By giving

* Lord Bacon.

power to those whose situation entitled them to it, and whose characters gave additional respect to the possession of it—and not exclusively to those whose corruption led them uniformly to barter every thing that could make their public characters respectable for the privilege of enjoying or dispensing it—they hoped to secure the approbation and support of the public, without having recourse to that system of corruption with which ministers had long been accustomed to influence it; and thus, while they flattered themselves that the measures they were pledged to pursue when they attained power, would increase the happiness of the people and the importance of the nation, they looked to their mode of conducting the government, as likely to introduce by example, as well as by precept, something more of purity of principle into the

degenerate

degenerate and habitually corrupt minds of the people.

Such were the benefits it was the uniform object of the only party which has existed in this country of late years united on principle, to secure to the nation; and such the means by which they at first proposed attaining them. But it was our misfortune that the power of satisfying the venality, which the practice of government had generated, daily increased; that the corrupt influence of the Crown became more and more extensive; that it decayed not with our danger, nor diminished with our decrease, but increased as our debt became oppressive, as the immediate expences of our government grew enormous. During the American war, the expenditure was so immense, that it afforded the means of almost unbounded influence;

So much so as to destroy all hopes that principle would be able gradually to supplant corruption; and it soon became apparent that there was a necessity for some immediate and forcible means of checking its progress, and diminishing its extent.

It was then that the party under Lord Rockingham, and those with whom they acted, brought forward and pledged themselves to the support of all those numerous regulations and reforms in the management of the government of the country, some of which they afterwards fortunately carried into execution; but in the opinion of many of the leading men amongst them, even these served only as temporary palliatives. Alive to a sense of the danger from that excessive venality which the practice of our constitution had produced, from the extravagant means of satisfying it which our calamities

lamities had created, they now regarded the limiting the power as inadequate at a time when the magnitude of the evil made it neceſſary, in part at leaſt, to root out the cauſes of its exiſtence.

They felt that there was no hope till the purity of the conſtituent body, and thereby that of their repreſentatives, ſhould be reſtored. Meetings were accordingly called, committees of correſpondence appointed, aſſociations formed, conventions of delegates from the different counties, cities, and towns, who had petitioned parliament, publicly held, with the approbation, concurrence and countenance of many of the firſt men of that party*; and before Lord Rockingham's

---

* Proofs of the Duke of Portland, Marquis of Rockingham, Lord Fitz-William, Mr. Thomas Grenville, Mr. Windham, Mr. Burke's having attended with aſſiduity the committees and aſſociations formed in the different

Ingham's acquisition of power, a discussion of the question of reform in the representation of parliament became one of their avowed objects. Mr. Pitt accordingly, in whose hands it was placed to be brought forward, soon after the formation of that administration, stated, " that the ministers
" had declared their virtuous resolution of
" supporting the king's government by
" means more honourable as well as more
" permanent than corruption; and the na-
" tion had confidence in the declaration of
" men who had so invariably proved them-
" selves the friends of freedom and the ani-

ferent counties, may be found in The Remembrancer: they are also much detailed in letters lately published in The Morning Chronicle under the signature of Hampden.

In the fourth article of the Protest entered in the Journals of the House of Lords, Feb. 8, 1780, there is an eloquent defence of the expediency and legality of Associations; amongst the signatures affixed to it, are to be found Portland, Devonshire, Richmond, Rockingham, Fitzwilliam, Temple, and Camden.

" mated

" mated supporters of an equal and fair sys-
" tem of representation *."

These were the objects that out of power they recommended, that in power they were pursuing, when the overturn of that admi-

* Mr. Pitt had then possibly seen a paper to this effect drawn up by the Duke of Richmond, the Marquis Rockingham, and the Marquis of Lansdown, and which, though not formally signed by them, was interchanged in their hand writings. Mr. Wyvill had also probably given him an account of the communication with Lord Rockingham, which he has since printed in his political papers. Lord Rockingham, having shewn him notes of the terms which his Majesty had acceded to before his coming into administration, stated, "that the Duke of
" Richmond on seeing the conditions above mentioned
" had observed, that no mention was made of a reform in
" parliament, and proposed, as an additional stipulation,
" that the discussion of that subject in parliament should
" be agreed to; which he Lord Rockingham consented
" to."

niftration, which the illnefs of Lord Rockingham perhaps retarded, which it certainly by no means contributed to, weakened for a time the Whig party. The avidity of fome to retain the power they had acquired, of others to poffefs themfelves of thofe fituations to which they afpired, in a confiderable degree diminifhed their numbers. But there never was more cordiality in principle than there exifted amongft thofe who perfevered in the objects of the party, and remained at this time united:—they had fhewn themfelves by experience to be animated with the fame ideas of public conduct; —they had done more, they had proved themfelves in practice capable of refifting the temptations of office and power, if not to be attained or retained by means which they confidered conftitutional. They had had opportunities for obfervation; and they were not so devoid of reflection, as not to have discovered that the path which Lord Auckland afterwards explored, through which Lord Loughborough marched, and into which so many chosen Whigs have lately walked, was the sure and immediate road to power. Ambitious however of the public welfare, they had long taught themselves to think that any view of individual ambition, or even a difference of opinion on any particular measure, was to be regarded as secondary to a perseverance in those principles, and in that system, which their creed led them to believe were the only security for the happiness of the people and the prosperity of the nation.

Such were the men, who, when admiring the virtues of Lord Rockingham, and regretting his death, looked to the Duke of Portland as likely from his character and virtues

virtues to fill the fituation with moſt credit to himſelf and advantage to the cauſe; and again erected under him the ſtandard of party, that they might continue to give to that fyſtem, and to thoſe meaſures which they had long purſued, the affiſtance and ſupport which party, by enabling them to call private honour and even views of intereſt in aid of public virtue, at all times ſecures.

Thus they remained united, ready as they always had been to receive affiſtance from all, reſolved, in the purſuit of the acquiſition or retaining of power by any other means, to give their ſupport to none *;—and it was

not

---

* Upon this is founded the diſtinction betwixt the two coalitions which the Duke of Portland has formed. In the firſt, he received the affiſtance of Lord North, to forward the views of the party, as was ſufficiently obvious

not long till Lord North's joining them produced (after a six weeks interregnum, employed in every endeavour at Court to avoid it) the necessity of forming an administration under the Duke of Portland, as first Lord of the Treasury. The intrigues however that took place to prevent its formation, were only a prelude to those that were resorted to to effect its dissolution;— and which terminated, after a fruitless attempt on the subject of the Prince's revenue, in the most open and scandalous exertion of the influence of the Crown, to defeat the measures of its ministers relative to the government of India. The effort was attended with success, the bill was thrown out in the House of Lords, and Mr. Pitt

vious from the opposition of the Court: in the last, he has lent his assistance to the support of that system and even of *that* administration which he had so often reprobated.

was brought forward as Minister: and whilst he was in private employed in corruptly lavishing every favour the Crown could bestow, to procure support, the friends of the Duke of Portland must now with shame remember, that in public, the favourite topics of his present colleague were the vice of an unprincipled coalition, and the imminent danger to the constitution from the prevalence of the aristocracy; that he then saw security alone in the unbridled efforts of a mob, or in the unrestrained exertions of that secret influence, to destroy which had been the constant object of the Whig party.

The mischief that seemed likely to attend this unlimited exercise of influence, this open corruption that then prevailed, was great; and as the impression of its fatal effects produced on those who then opposed him

was ſtrong, ſo the diſapprobation in the pub‑
lic correſpondence of the Duke of Portland
at their head was marked.

To ſee, to ſpeak, to treat with the Miniſter
whilſt he retained the ſituation which he
had thus unconſtitutionally acquired, was
deemed and ſtated to be a dereliction of
principle *; and virtually to involve the
surrender

* Extract of a Letter from the Duke of Portland to
Thomas Groſvenor, Eſq. Chairman of the Members of
the Houſe of Commons met at the St. Alban's Ta‑
vern, dated

" Devon Houſe, Saturday 31 Jan. 1784.

" I believe you will agree, that the continuance of
" the preſent Miniſtry, and the honour of the Houſe of
" Commons, are not very eaſily reconcilable."

Extract of a Letter from Ditto to Ditto.

" Monday morning, 2d February, 1784.
" I very ſincerely regret that the expedient to which
" I referred ſhould be thought inapplicable to the diffi‑
" culties

surrender of every tenet relative to the Conſtitution, which as Whigs they had maintained.

" culties I had ſtated. I certainly ſuggeſted it as a
" mode of reſignation the leaſt embarraſſing to Govern-
" ment, in the ordinary functions of office, and, at the
" ſame time, as a proof of a diſpoſition to conſult the
" honour of the Houſe of Commons, as it ſtands pledged
" by the Reſolution of the 16th January. *This laſt*
" *is a preliminary, which, as a friend to the ſpirit of the*
" *Conſtitution, I muſt think myſelf bound invariably to*
" *require.*

" With reſpect to myſelf, I am willing to hope, that
" I have not been miſtaken in the conception I formed
" of your wiſhes, by ſuppoſing that it was with Mr.
" Pitt that you were deſirous I ſhould have a liberal and
" unreſerved intercourſe, and not with the head of an
" Adminiſtration to which I was *merely to bring an*
" *acceſſion of ſtrength.* But Mr. Pitt's meſſage places
" him in another character; *and your own good ſenſe*
" *will readily ſuggeſt to you, that it was impoſſible for*
" *me to ſuppoſe that your expectations extended to a confi-*
" *dential*

maintained.—As things were then situated, it was not however to be expected, that corruption would not privately produce its effect. Many of those who had joined under Lord North, had been too long accustomed to the system that prevailed when he formerly conducted the government, to suppose that it would not be attended with success; it in reality soon diminished the numbers of Opposition; and, aided by the clamour which was every where prevalent at the general election that ensued, established that majority which has since supported the Minister.

"dential conference with him as the representative of the
"present Administration.

"If I had done this, I must have fallen in your esteem
"(which I assure you is a very serious object to me), as
"I should have shewn myself insensible of what is due to
"the House of Commons."

But

But it left the Duke of Portland at the head of a party (in refpect of numbers and ability, more powerful than the hiftory of the country antecedently furnifhed any example of) bound to fupport the meafures of Lord Rockingham, with the additional pledge of refraining from all connection with thofe concerned in the late intrigue for power, till by relinquifhing their fituations, thus improperly obtained, they had in a degree wiped away that injury which the conftitution was fuppofed to have fuftained from their conduct.

For years the Minifter retained his majority; and the party, though individuals might differ about particular meafures, remained united, maintained their principle, and purfued their fyftem. Their ftrength and ability were fuch as feemed likely ultimately to enfure fuccefs; and whilft it thus created

created a doubt in the minds of all, whether they offered up the fureſt ſacrifice to their venality, by conſulting their immediate or their remote intereſts, it encouraged the public to ſpeak out its mind upon the important queſtions that occurred; and in many inſtances gave that efficacy to their opinion, even when hinted, which, without the exiſtence of ſuch a party, it would have been in vain in the ſituation of the country to have expected. Of this, during the courſe of theſe laſt ten years, there have been many examples; none however more marked than that which took place on the recent inſtance of the Ruſſian armament; on which occaſion the miniſtry were induced haſtily to relinquiſh their meaſures, in a manner as diſgraceful to themſelves as it was probably fortunate for their country; in a manner, however, which, as it contributed in no ſmall degree to weaken and de-

grade

grade in public eftimation thofe who conducted the government of the country, fo it added both in ftrength and popularity to their opponents.

Such was the fituation of thofe concerned in the politics of this country at the commencement of the year 1792. The revolution in France, though it had engaged the attention of all, though the opinions entertained of it were known to be various, when alluded to in public, feemed to be confidered univerfally as likely to fecure to this country a certainty of peace and tranquillity.

Mr. Burke alone had at that time viewed it as pregnant with immediate calamity; he had twice introduced the difcuffion in Parliament, in a manner that was deemed by thofe who had long loved him and wifhed

to

to repress it, disorderly; by those who had long shewn their aversion to him, and who, now wished mischievously to encourage him, indiscreet:—but he was openly supported in his opinions by none; and it seemed improbable, that what was universally deemed the folly of one man should become the politics of all. Through life he had displayed talents that deservedly commanded admiration; but his want of judgment and feeling had so enfeebled their effect, that whether he was employed in hurling his Sovereign in the hour of calamity from the throne, in brandishing a Jacobin dagger in the senate, or in bespeaking the favour of the court for the criminal he was about to accuse; by the ill-judged coarse invective in which he indulged, the best exertions of his talents were no longer received but with a mixture of pity on the part of his

his friends, and contempt on the part of his opponents. His opinions, and even his exertions in public, had been through life attended with much unmerited unpopularity; and it seemed therefore hardly possible, that at a moment when (to use his own language) he had so softened, diluted, blended, and weakened, the distinguishing colours of his life, as to leave nothing distinct or determinate behind — that he should be able to sow the seeds of the remote dissolution of that party, which perhaps he had long injured by his support;— or that his writings, to the misfortune of his country, would be in future resorted to as the only grammar that contains the elements of the present politics of the nation.

But as party has always been the most formidable check upon those who have acquired power by intrigue, and retained it by by corruption; to divide and difunite has ever been their moſt eager purfuit, and the flighteſt opportunity was too valuable to be loſt. Nothing could difplay this in ſtronger colours than the anxiety of the adherents of Adminiſtration to promote Mr. Burke's being allowed to difcufs the French revolution in the committee on the Quebec Bill; —and the hopes of future fupport artfully thrown out upon that occafion by the Miniſter himfelf, to a man whom he had ever antecedently treated with haughty contempt, exhibited a ſtrong proof of the fatisfaction he derived even from the moſt diſtant hopes of creating difunion, but proceeded probably more from a compliance with the general fyſtem of conduct to be purfued, than from any expectation that yet dawned upon him of being able through fuch a medium to effect the difunion of his opponents.

It

It was not however long before a more flattering opportunity prefented itfelf. Early in this year, a conviction that the abufes in France had been fuffered to gather and accumulate until nothing but an eruption could put an end to them, and that preventative remedies had not been thought of in time, or were not propofed until it was too late to carry them into effect, induced many belonging to the party to think, that the experience of the day now taught them to look to a reform in Parliament as more than ever defirable. Lord Chatham had ftated it " as neceffary to infufe a portion of new " health into the Conftitution," and had declared, " that in his opinion, without it, this " nation, with the beft capacities for grandeur " and happinefs of any on the face of the " earth, muft be confounded with the mafs " of thofe whofe liberties were loft in the " corruption of the people." Many of the

minifters

ministers had formerly supported it;—the leading man in opposition had been active in committees and associations to promote it;—Lord Rockingham, antecedent to coming into administration, had formally adopted it;—and the prospect of peace and tranquillity, held out by those in power as certain, seemed to point out the time as peculiarly adapted to it. They had seen in France, that as government was gradually weakened it had been reduced from bargaining with the people to yield to them: and they conceived, that now, when the Constitution was rooted in the affections of almost all, was the only time when you could attempt to perpetuate the attachment to it, by giving to the people that weight to which in the eyes of most they seemed according to the spirit of our Constitution to be entitled.

From the Minister they had every reason to expect support to a measure which has been emphatically styled the legacy of his dying father, and his own virgin effort;—from some of the heads of the party with whom they were connected they knew they would meet with opposition; but they could not expect a very eager or ardent resistance of measures which they themselves had formerly with such activity pursued: and as the difference of opinion upon the subject of parliamentary reform was known; as it was understood, and in a manner explained *, that it never could

* At a meeting at Burlington House, in the beginning of March 1792, for the purpose of consulting on a measure that was then to be brought forward, parliamentary reform was openly stated to be a subject on which there were known to exist three separate and distinct opinions in the party. But this was never considered as a ground of disunion.

tend

tend to the difunion of the party, they at all events faw no danger of depriving the country of the fure benefits which were likely to flow from it.

When, however, a notice was given on the fubject in the Houfe of Commons; regardlefs of his former conduct, the Minifter fhewed himfelf fo eager, that in a manner unufual, and even diforderly *, he retracted his former opinions on the fubject, invidioufly connected the propofal with an intention of exciting in this country a revolution fimilar to that in France; and with triumphant applaufe announced his apoftacy: it was a fubject on which he had formerly been oppofed by many of thofe

---

* To debate a fubject upon a notice given, and when of courfe there can be no queftion before the Houfe, has always been deemed in Parliament irregular.

who acted with the present Opposition, and on which he was sure to obtain his favourite object of dividing the strength of that party which he now more than ever dreaded: he remembered the line they had formerly taken too well to doubt that numbers of them would give his new opinions their decided support; and if to the prospect of such a division his own consistency seemed to him then but a poor sacrifice, the opportunity afforded by a declaration in debate of their being ready to concert measures with him, must have indeed amply compensated for any loss of character which in his estimation he was likely to sustain, and was a thing not to be neglected by a Minister, whose friends will find it difficult to prove that he has not on the subject of reform listened with as much attention to betray, as he has spoken with assiduity to deceive.

To force on the queſtion of reform itſelf was impoſſible; the notice had been given for the following ſeſſion of Parliament: but in the courſe of the diſcuſſion that had taken place, the love of French principles, the reſolutions of certain ſocieties, and the doctrines of ſome pamphlets that had been circulated, had been ſo artfully blended with the ſubject of reform, that the pledge given to unite and conſult on the one was conceived to extend to the other.

Even upon thoſe ſubjects, to deviſe a queſtion that could be brought forward with honour to himſelf, and with advantage to his country, was difficult; but it was at that moment too deſirable not at all events to be attempted.—By means of a proclamation, and a propoſed addreſs of thanks,

thanks, a measure was therefore soon contrived, which carried internal evidence of its being brought forward with no other view than invidiously to attempt to separate those who had been so long connected. To promote that end it was admirably calculated; it was projected the moment there appeared the most remote probability of creating it; —as devised to produce the real effect intended, it commanded admiration;—but the impudence of the attempt would have startled any one less practised in the arts of delusion than those by whom it was framed. No ostensible ground that it held forth could reasonably account for its appearance at the moment. It alone stated the existence of publications that had been openly circulated for a length of time, of writings industriously recommending them that were not new to the public eye; and it hinted

at

at the danger of societies whose resolutions had long been openly advertised. The resorting to so extraordinary a measure seemed a declaration of the inadequacy of that constitution, which they held out to our admiration, to protect itself by the usual provisions of its laws. It in a manner recorded their past inattention to the dangers which they then deprecated; and confessed their inability to discharge the ordinary duties of their station without the extraordinary aid of Parliament; and it seemed likely, by the weakness and inefficiency which it exhibited in his Majesty's councils, to be more derogatory from the just authority of government than any imaginary progress, which with great injustice to a loyal people they attributed to the principles asserted in the writings of which they complained. But these dangers to the peace of the community

munity were regarded as trifling; the indirect avowal of incapacity and inconfiftency appeared to the Minifter fmall, when compared to the finifter advantages that attended a meafure which held out the fure profpect of producing private confultation and communication with thofe with whom whilft in office he had eight years before, in vain, endeavoured to obtain it, and of creating at once difunion where for eight years he had in vain attempted to fow the feeds of it.

He had alternately courted popularity and Court favour, as means of obtaining power *. He had conjoined both to fecure

* In his oppofition to the American war, and bringing on the queftion of reform, he feems to have aimed at the one; and, in coming into office after Lord Rockingham's death, to have taken advantage of the other.

it ;

it *; but in abjuring that reform in the reprefentation, the ground on which he had aimed at acquiring the one, he feemed to have diminifhed his chance of popular fupport, as much as his recently infifting on his Sovereign's difmiffing Lord Thurlow muft have diminifhed his claim to the other. And he now therefore more than ever looked to the difmemberment of his opponents, and the poffible chance of acquiring by that means fome new fupport, as the object which ought, and in reality did, direct all his meafures.

That the proclamation was by the Minifter himfelf confidered as a meafure of private expediency, and not of State neceffity, can hardly be doubted. In any other

---

* When he became firft Lord of the Treafury.

point

point of view there could have existed no necessity of consultation with Burlington-House; he required not the addition of their numbers; his triumphant and confiding majority still remained; he was still surrounded by the protecting influence of those who had supported him since he was at the helm of affairs; he had in his hands the full means of carrying his measures into effect; and without consultation he was already secure of the voice of those who had listened to him with approbation on the notice given of a motion for reform.

To open the door to private negotiation with them must have been his aim. If he as Minister really thought it necessary to adopt measures for repressing a spirit of insurrection in the country — what were these measures? Was the proclamation the only

only one he at this time propofed? Had he no idea of then calling out the militia, and of other meafures he has fince adopted? Or was no fuch intimation given to Burlington-Houfe? Is it not notorious that they acquiefced in the firft part of his propofal, and rejected the reft? and that in compliance with the opinion of men no ways connected with the executive adminiftration of the country, and in no degree refponfible for its effects, the Minifter laid afide meafures he himfelf had ftated as neceffary for the public good?—that the militia remained quiet? and that the proclamation, cut and carved into a different fhape by the ftill fqueamifh followers of the Duke of Portland in his new purfuit, was deemed fufficient by Mr. Pitt, becaufe it was fatisfactory to them? If he was in earneft therefore in his belief of danger, to his private ends he

facrificed

sacrificed the interests of his country. If his dreads were assumed, we see in this early stage a self-evident proof of that system of conduct he has since for similar purposes invariably pursued—wisely perhaps for his private ends, but unfortunately with too much success for the welfare of his country.

By the first appearances that attended this attempt to divide, he had no reason to be discouraged; the proclamation produced both private consultation with him and public difference of opinion in his opponents. But to those who at private meetings heard the strong declarations of adherence to the system on which the party was founded, and of undiminished enmity to the principles on which the administration was formed, and had been conducted[*],

there

[*] Before the debate on the proclamation, a meeting was

there appeared little prospect of his ultimately effecting any coalition. And even their public language must have afforded him but a discouraging prospect: he could hardly imagine that the Viceroy of Corsica could be induced to wave differences that were fundamental and irreconcileable *; or that Mr. Windham would soon strip himself of his embroidered suit of pretence, and share with him the tattered

was held at Mr. Fox's of all those in Opposition who were likely to take part in the debate on either side, for the purpose of communicating the line they intended following in debate, and thus marking in the strongest possible manner the impracticability of its creating disunion.

* Words used by Sir Gilbert Elliott, in a speech which, as it appeared to have been written, must have been studied.

rags

rags of his genuine deformity; that he could be prevailed upon to exhibit himself in conjunction with him before a confiding majority, like the uncased Frenchman in ruffles without a shirt—in tinsel and lace on the outside, and in dirt and dowlas within*: and the declaration made in debate by the Duke of Portland himself, did not seem to be calculated to give him much encouragement. As he had prevailed however in establishing a private communication on the subject of the proclamation, in a manner contradictory to the antecedent declarations of the party, he felt doubtless to a degree encouraged by a channel being

---

* See Mr. Windham's Speech on Mr. Thompson's motion, " To inquire into all abuses committed by per-" sons in office at the election of a Member to serve in " Parliament for the City of Westminster, in July 1788 " —as far as the same relates to penalties incurred un-" der the Excise Laws, or Lottery Act."

now

now for the first time opened, through which an experiment might be made.

That the Minister should sacrifice one of the main props of his government to the unnatural object of providing for one whom he had ever reprobated, and by whom he had been uniformly, with acrimony, opposed, seemed strange; that at the moment of holding forth in public the necessity of supporting and strengthening the hand of government, he himself should choose to overturn one of the principal pillars by which his power had been supported, was singular. But his plan was now obviously concerted;— the apparent division of Opposition had disclosed to him new views of personal greatness: with the subtilty he has ever possessed, he grasped at the opening; and to add to the probability of its success, disregarding what must have been the feelings of his Sovereign,

Sovereign, and forgetful of the fervices he had rendered, by the difmiffion of Lord Thurlow a door was opened to the completion of the views of the man in Oppofition that he muft have regarded as moft likely to liften to his offers. He recollected the conduct of Mr. Wedderburn, when he became Solicitor General; and if he did not augur from thence a probability of fucceeding in detaching Lord Loughborough and fome of his friends from the party, he faw at leaft upon this occafion the certainty of finding in him a fure and willing negotiator. He had probably read with attention the works of his new mafter in politics, and the declaration had not efcaped him, that " as to " leaders in parties, there is nothing more " common than to fee them blindly led; it " is by go-betweens the world is governed: " thefe go-betweens influence the perfons " with whom they carry on the intercourfe,

4 " by

" by ftating their own fenfe to each of them
" as the fenfe of the other." And thus indeed they generally obtain their ends. As long as the Chancellorfhip was vacant, he could have no doubt that the ends of the Chief Juftice of the Common Pleas would coincide accurately with his own; he was fure of his activity;—and the general difpofition he had at the time to believe every thing Mr. Burke faid, gave him perhaps hopes of the fuccefs of fuch a go-between.

After fome fruitlefs efforts and vague converfation, however, in which the arts incident to the fituation were doubtlefs not left unpractifed by the ingenuity of the negociator, the attempt proved abortive; and even the conductor of the negociation himfelf feemed to have caught for a moment a little of the principle which thofe with whom he negociated then poffeffed, and declared

clared his unwillingness without their concurrence to accept.

By the Duke of Portland so little attention was paid to it, that almost at the very time a proposition was made, with his concurrence and authority, by a person deservedly high in rank and estimation, for the formation of a new administration *; and so little did Mr. Pitt's friends see any hopes of acquiring new strength, or any certainty of stability, that, it is said, they forced him soon after this to throw aside that affected squeamishness which formerly distinguished his conduct, and accept the Wardenship of the Cinque Ports, as a permanent provision in the event of a reverse of fortune.

But the autumn of this year was replete

---

* The Duke of Leeds is supposed to have had the honour of submitting this proposal to his Majesty.

with more extraordinary events than in the history of man were ever antecedently crowded together in so short a period of time. If those who were avowed enemies, in speculation, to the French revolution felt elated when they saw the rapid progress of the allied arms on their entering into France, the subsequent occurrences had tended equally to depress them; and as the exertions of the French made in their defence commanded respect, it was by them dreaded, that their principles would in this country immediately acquire a proportionable admiration. Reason had so far deceived all concerning the events of the campaign, that it became for a time out of fashion to resort to it. Those who formerly represented themselves as fearing that change might lead to stir up an admiration of French principles, and for that reason more than ever disliking reform, now openly avowed their dread of an immediate revolution; and to their imaginations, occupied with the phantom, there was hardly any occurrence that did not appear somehow to portend it: with perfect indifference to the reality of the grounds of their fears, like true zealots, they thought and they harangued alone on the extent of their alarms.

The French in the mean time, elated with their success, had wantonly in several instances been guilty of acts which gave us just ground of offence; and the Minister, whilst the feelings and temper of those who had formerly joined him upon the proclamation seemed upon these topics to insure him support, saw the certainty of being able, in consequence of the conduct of France, to produce discussion on the subject.

He now saw a prospect of division, not upon one isolated measure, but upon questions

tions which, as long as they were under difcuffion, muft from their nature form the moft important fubjects of deliberation, and thus of creating amongft his opponents fuch a difference, as a man even lefs experienced in thofe arts than himfelf could eafily forefee would at leaft give an opportunity, and furnifh ample pretence, for the many who were attached alone by feelings of honour to the party (he had fhewn himfelf fo anxious, by divifion, to deftroy), to confult thofe views of intereft which the poffeffion of his fituation has taught others as well as himfelf to believe exifted in all.

If the interefts of his country had been his only or his principal object; if he had been alone actuated with a defire to obtain redrefs for the injury or infult that we or our allies might have fuffered; as there exifts no means of obtaining fuch redrefs but by

addreffing

addressing ourselves to the power of whom we complain, he would of course have attempted to negociate. Then was not the moment when he would have roused a question about the recognition of the French Republic, which by his conduct he had already decided*; or when he would have laid such a stress upon the difference betwixt a secret and avowed negociator—a point which, though it seemed immaterial to us, the nature of their situation, he knew, rendered it impossible for the Provisional Executive Government to get over †. Then was not the

---

* See Mr. Fox's Letter to his Constituents.

† In a conversation Mr. Pitt had with M. Maret, the end of November 1792, the latter reports himself to have said, "You speak, Sir, of a secret agent. I "foresee a difficulty.—You know that in France we "profess a great respect for the public opinion, which "constitutes

the time, when he would have ſtated with ſuch alarm, and ſhewn ſuch eagerneſs to reſent with acrimony, communications of the French with ſocieties in this country, which he had long ſuffered unmoleſted to proceed *. But in purſuit of his favourite object, the

" conſtitutes the force of free government, and which
" is a wholeſome reſtraint on thoſe who govern. This
" public opinion, however, is ready to demand of
" the Proviſional Executive Council, Why it has had
" the weakneſs not to require the recognition of the
" French Republic by England? Will it then be poſſible
" to treat with you by the means of a ſecret agent?
" We have here a Miniſter Plenipotentiary, who has
" all the confidence of our Government."

* See the correſpondence of the Conſtitutional Society with the Convention of France and various Jacobin Clubs, publiſhed in London in 1792, where there is to be found an account of the reception of an embaſſy from the Jacobin Society of Nantes, and a number of letters, of a date much antecedent to this, ſtronger than any thing that has appeared.

division of his opponents and the acquisition of supporters, this was obviously the only line he could pursue. Looking to it, he was naturally led to throw such difficulties in the way of accommodation, to suspend with as much art as possible negociation, that the object of difference might be kept up; and to call Parliament together as soon as possible, that the opportunity of fermenting it by public discussion might occur. Under the laws of the country, it was difficult to meet Parliament so soon as the eagerness in his favourite pursuit rendered desirable; but the object was too big for even the greatest obstacles not to appear insignificant. At any other time, he would have been careful of the facts he put into the mouth of his Sovereign; but to obtain his end, he hesitated not now to issue a proclamation, which, as it gave the first, fortunately gave the last account

count of any infurrections exifting *; and in confequence of this, Parliament, as the law directs, was immediately fummoned.

In anticipating the fupport which he was now fure in Parliament of obtaining, he was not dead to a fenfe of the neceffity of roufing a fudden fermentation in the minds of the people, that they might fympathize with the conduct which his purpofes rendered it neceffary he fhould purfue. To introduce any thing like that club government which had

---

* Mr. Grenville, who on the firft proclamation fupported and ftill fupports Adminiftration, declared, "that nothing that had been mentioned appeared to "him by any means equivalent to an infurrection. He "was of opinion, that the ftate of the country was ill "defcribed by the proclamation; and he was the more "induced to come forward with this opinion, as he was "apprehenfive that danger might arife from fuch ex-"aggeration."

been

been the fource of calamity in France feemed a ftrange and dangerous meafure, at a moment when his eloquence was chiefly to be employed in reprobating it. But, in purfuit of his ends, he had become habitually negligent of the confequences or the means : and as he was ready to rifque the involving us in war, by the haughty language he held, and the difficulties he artfully created, for the purpofe of flattering thofe in Parliament whofe fupport he courted; fo he was willing to adopt even the hated forms of French anarchy, to force the minds of the people into fuch a ftate, as might admit of their fympathizing with thofe meafures, which his intrigue for fupporters had induced him fo fuddenly and rapidly to adopt, that the ufual fure but flow channels of influence had not time to effect the change which his fecurity required. Clubs accordingly everywhere appeared, headed by the dependants

and

and established under the influence of Government, and the clamour that was raised soon announced the success of the measure. When Parliament met, the result of his plans was apparent. In the party he wished to break down there existed a marked division; and as the disunion furnished the opportunity, the clamour of the country soon gave encouragement to all those who were withheld only by a slight feeling of honour, to declare their support of his measures. It was then that affected dread of the friends of the unfortunate Brissot producing an apparent neglect of his engagements to his own, gave to the nation a new Chancellor *, and to the Minister additional support. And the successive compliments, which by the Alien Bill, the infractions of the Commercial Treaty, and the ignomini-

* In the House of Lords, the dread of the friends of Brissot was the satisfactory reason given for his conduct.

ously dismissing the Ambassador, he paid to his new supporters, whilst they unfortunately involved us in a war, of which, six months before this opportunity of acquiring strength occurred, he had hardly seen in fifteen years the probability, insured him the promised support even of some of the leaders of the party, at the moment that he was risking the safety of his country to rob them of their strength.

The strong and animated exertions of the small Opposition that remained to promote negociation and secure peace, which undoubtedly then might have been obtained *,

* I had at this time frequent opportunities of seeing and talking with many of the leading men in France; and my observation concurs with the account since given by Dumourier, and even with that given by a man supposed to be in the employ of Government, to convince me that there existed not an individual in that country, in possession of any influence, who did not anxiously wish to avoid hostilities with this.

were

were overborne by the strength he had acquired, and drowned in the clamour he had created... And whilst I look back with sorrow at the support which Mr. Fox then lost; with pride at the measures he recommended; with astonishment at the success of the intrigue of the Minister for supporters; with grief at the calamities it has occasioned—I cannot help recollecting the criticism of Lord Bacon on the speech of Themistocles the Athenian, which emphatically describes the different excellencies those statesmen exhibited upon this, as they have upon every other occasion. " Themistocles
" being desired at a feast to touch a lute, said
" he could not; but yet he could make a
" small town a great city. These words
" (holpen a little with a metaphor) may
" express two different abilities in those that
" deal in business of estate:—for if a true
" survey be taken of counsellors and statesmen,

"men, there may be found, though rarely,
"those that can make a small state great,
"yet cannot fiddle;—as on the other side
"there will be found a great many that can
"fiddle very cunningly, but yet are so far
"from being able to make a small state great,
"as their gift lies the other way, to bring a
"great and flourishing state to ruin and de-
"cay:—and certainly those degenerate arts
"and shifts, whereby many counsellors and
"governors gain both favour with their
"master and estimation with the vulgar, de-
"serve no better name than fiddling."

By the art of Mr. Pitt and the folly of some of its leaders, Opposition was now effectually fiddled out of most of its supporters *; by his conduct and measures the country

---

* When the Duke of Portland called, in the month of

country was involved in war; and thus, without an attempt at, and even by means of carefully avoiding, negociation, the different ends of all were attained. The Court saw that party broken down, whose opposition to the system of ruling by secret influence they dreaded, and which it had been the Minister's object at all events to demolish. The Duke of Portland and his friends saw the country involved in that war, in which their alarms foolishly taught them to see the security and prosperity of the nation.

Deprived of their strength, it was in vain that the Duke of Portland, and some few of February following, a meeting of all those who had formerly acted in the Opposition, to consider the means of opposing the Traitorous Correspondence Bill (which he however afterwards supported), excepting those who with Mr. Fox opposed the war, and some of his Grace's own relations, there was hardly any body attended.

of the leading men with whom he was connected, ſtill to a degree maintained the principle upon which they had acted; that they repeated their averſion to the ſyſtem upon which adminiſtration had been formed, and attributed to that, and the conduct of the miniſters, the calamities in which the country was involved; that upon all occaſions, both in public and in private, they held out the impoſſibility of ſuch a coalition *. The opinion of the Miniſter,
which

---

* In the Houſe of Lords, on the Alien Bill, the Duke of Portland declared, that " it was not on account " of any perſonal attachment to the preſent Adminiſtra- " tion that he ſupported it. He could not forget the " manner in which they came into power; he could not " forget the many circumſtances in their conduct by " which, in his opinion, they had forfeited all title to " the confidence of the nation ; he could not forget that " to their miſconduct many of our preſent difficulties " were owing."---And in the Houſe of Commons Lord Titchfield, after declaring that his political ſentiments

and

which they formerly poſſeſſed, and even now ſtated, one would have thought muſt have taught them, that ſuch declarations could now alone ſerve as food for his vanity; that he muſt have looked with delight at the ſtate into which he had reduced them—with joy at the ſituation in which he had placed himſelf. If the war was attended with ſucceſs, he ſaw himſelf ſecure of their ſupport, ſure of monopolizing the credit—and, if unfortunately it ſhould be otherwiſe, he eaſily muſt have perceived,

and attachments remained the ſame that they had ever been. " His opinion of the gentlemen who compoſed
" the preſent Adminiſtration was in no reſpect altered;"
ſtated that " he could not too explicitly declare, that in
" no other reſpect could he give them any ſhare of his
" confidence, and that he could not too openly avow his
" attachment to thoſe political principles and connec-
" tions, with which he had the happineſs of entering
" into public life, and to which it was his ſincere
" wiſh for ever to adhere."

O

from

from the experience he now had of them, that it would require less management than he had already practised with certainty, to share with them the disgrace and divide the responsibility. Ever fond of humbling those with whom he unites, with what pleasure must he have heard those declarations, when he anticipated the additional ignominy that would attend their conduct if ever the hour came when the misfortunes of the country should render a union convenient for him! for he could not doubt but that, at any time, he had them completely in his power; and that a call upon their honour to come forward, and share the responsibility in conducting those measures of which they had in a manner been the authors, even if their inclination for place did not make them grasp at the offer, would probably effect that which however at all events a threat of his retiring was sure to secure.

In

In the hour of calamity we have accordingly seen them brought forward; and as their folly had already effected a sacrifice of the strength of the party to his art, they have now been forced to offer up the principle of it to his convenience. The term is harsh, and I feel perhaps more in writing it than most of them will in reading it; but whilst truth prevents me from distinguishing betwixt Mr. Eden and the Duke of Portland, I learn, from recollection, that there was a time in which he would have felt it as strongly as myself.

Yet ingenuity itself cannot draw any material distinction; the very principle of the party, as it precluded its dissolution by difference on any particular measure, rendered it impracticable to coalesce with an administration formed on the principle of Mr. Pitt's, even though you agreed with him

him on fubjects of the greateft importance. The cordial fupport of Mr. Fox on the queftion of the Slave Trade never had made a union more probable; but if it was otherwife, Lord Auckland would ftand armed with his defence as well as the Duke of Portland: and the defence of both is fimilar; for if the one confiders the war as a cafe of fufficient importance to authorize it, the other may confider the commercial treaty as fuch. The language of both conveys the fame idea, and is equally repugnant to every principle on which they were united: it makes the ftability of connection depend upon the whim, caprice, perhaps the convenience, of individuals, and deftroys every ground on which a party can exift.

Such is the manner and fuch the purpofes for which this country has in reality been involved in war; and such are the *means* that have induced some of the leading men of that party, which it had been the object and the pride of Lord Rockingham's life to form, to trample its principles under foot, and thus to give Mr. Pitt an opportunity of completing his triumph over them—who, as he had formerly exhibited Lord Auckland on the treasury bench—now reserved for the head of the Whigs, the more marked humiliation of exhibiting him in that cabinet whose formation he had uniformly deprecated, decorated with that blue ribbon which his Sovereign and the Nation claimed for Lord Howe, and in possession of that third Secretaryship of State which it had been the boast of his party formerly to reform*.

Thus

---

* In Lord Rockingham's administration, this office was abolished, and an Act of Parliament passed to make

Thus terminated, in form as well as reality, the exifting Whig party: affording, unfortunately for the country, a ftriking leffon to men of talents and abilities in future, how they lend thefe ineftimable bleffings, where political fear may predominate or folly may guide. Happy in domeftic life, beloved by their friends, and refpected by all, the nominal heads of the party might have long, with credit to themfelves, enjoyed the tranquil comforts that fortune and rank could give. But, drawn from their natural fphere, pufhed into public notice, raifed in the opinion of

it untenable with a feat in the Houfe of Commons. In the perfon of the Duke of Portland it has been revived, who has lent himfelf to a miferable evafion of the fpirit of the Act, and, though in poffeffion of the department held by Mr. Dundas, has, by accepting the feals that were formerly in the poffeffion of the third Secretary, fecured, as they imagine under the letter of the Act, the poffibility of Mr. Dundas's remaining in Parliament.

the

the world by the talents and abilities of those around them—at the moment when these by steadiness and principle saw, in the preservation of the country from the calamities in which it was about to be involved, an ample requital for their past toils—at a time when party became most necessary—some actuated by fear, some by folly, at once annihilated all their fair hopes. By his arts they were induced to throw themselves at the feet of a Minister whom they had reprobated, and by this shameful and disastrous event have for the time, it is to be feared, rendered it equally impossible for the Sovereign on the one hand, or the Public on the other, to resist the calamity of the measures he has, to secure their support, been induced to adopt.

Of the effects of the war I have already had occasion to state much to you; on the conduct of it, and the increased calamities that are likely in future to attend it, I shall in my next have an opportunity of observing. Of the immediate effect of the dissolution of the Whig party, we have had some small specimens. In the unparalleled provision of the traitorous correspondence bill; in the doctrines held relative to voluntary contributions, and the admitting of foreign troops; in the suspension of the Habeas Corpus Act, we feel its effects. What will be the ultimate consequence it is hardly possible to say; but there is no one can see with indifference—none who have reflected seriously on the nature of the government of this country, without dread, indeed—*party*, the only engine which enabled you to combine all the passions and feelings of men, in aid of public virtue against that prevalent venality generated by the practice of our constitution, so weakened and diminished at a

moment

moment when corruption is enabled to make its moſt dangerous efforts—" when its mo-
" dern improved arts, by contracts, ſubſcrip-
" tions, and jobs, is attended with this per-
" verſe and vexatious conſequence, that their
" benefit is not only unconnected with that of
" the nation, but grows under diſtreſs; when
" thoſe around the Miniſter* feed on the ex-
" pence, and fatten on every extravagance
" that art and ill conduct can engraft on the
" natural diſadvantages of remote, raſh, ill-
" fated, impolitic and unſucceſsful war; and
" when the Miniſter's direct intereſt requires
" him to purſue a deſperate game, and even
" in ſelf-defence to increaſe that very expence
" which is his crime; to entrench himſelf
" ſtill deeper in corruption, and by headlong

---

* It is believed, that the fees upon the treaties and the commiſſions have increaſed the emoluments of ſome of the Offices of State to an extent of which there is no experience.

" and

" and unmeafured extravagance to have the
" means of juftifying to the faithful Com-
" mons the events which his plans have oc-
" cafioned."

There is one confequence, however, which from all this muft but too furely follow, more particularly if it is true, that there is at this moment a difinclination to fubordination.—As long as public virtue diftinguifhed the Minifters and furrounded the Throne, the libels of a Paine might be regarded with indifference; but when the firft favours of the Court involve uniformly a dereliction of principle upon the part of the man who receives them, then it is that, if there exifts any thing like virtue in the community, it muft take from thofe around the King the regard of the People.—When honours are feldom acquired, but with the lofs of character,

racter, then it is that they generate contempt more than they command refpect.——— When public virtue is no longer to be found amongft public men, then it is that public inftitutions can no longer obtain that reverence the welfare of the community requires.

The fituation of affairs, in whatever point of view they are confidered, offers, it muft be acknowledged, but a melancholy and gloomy profpect to the eye. It cannot be fuppofed, that a perfon can feel otherwife than in a degree difgufted with all political purfuits, when he reflects that thofe he had for years fondly hoped would have been the inftruments of the falvation of the country, have been the means of bringing it into its prefent fituation—when he knows not whether moft to deplore the reduction, and in a manner the annihilation of the party he has supported, or the fatal effects of the measures to which its destruction has led. There remains to me, however, one satisfaction, that of thinking that as an individual I have conducted myself firmly, honestly, and conscientiously. Prudently for my personal views, in the sense of the word arising out of the corruption of the country, I pretend not to have acted; by the dictates of sound wisdom it would be presumption in me to say I have been guided; but to the merit of consistency I must put in my claim; and I may venture, I think, to assert, that what was in me the effect of early conviction, has been now for many years the uniform source of my political action.

In that line I must persevere:—reduced as the party with which I act is in numbers, still I for one shall never despair: in the justice

of

of our cause I feel our strength; in the talents and abilities of those with whom I have the honour to act, our main support.

It is our object to recover to this country the blessings of tranquillity and peace; we wish to put an end to the irritation of the public mind; we look with anxiety to the restitution of the mild practice of English law; we wish not to hazard the blessings we enjoy in a contest with what we are taught to consider the miseries of France.

To obtain these points, however desirable and necessary for the country, may be difficult, but I trust not impossible; the public mind must in time be undeceived; reflection must operate a change in the opinions of men; it cannot be long ere the people will begin to think what they can gain! and what they may lose!

Southend, October 7, 1794.

LETTER

LETTER III.

I HAVE already laid before you what appear to me to have been the real causes of our present unfortunate situation; I have submitted to your consideration the principles that, in my mind, have guided the conduct of Ministers; and I have endeavoured to shew you, that no regard to the public, but an attention to private and particular interests, has led us on from step to step to the present scene of accumulated distress. It now remains to give you a view of our present and future prospects; and as I have explained my past, so will I now shortly consider what must be my future line of political conduct, which, as it is guided chiefly by principle, no change of circumstances

circumstances can materially affect, and no unforeseen occurrence can greatly alter. Easy and simple indeed will this last task prove, when compared with the difficulty of conjecturing any possible mode in which the present Ministers can with honour extricate themselves or their country from the unheard-of and unsurmountable calamities in which we are involved. The prosperity of the country might perhaps under different men, and by pursuing different measures, still be preserved; but for Ministers to undo every thing they have done, to unsay all they have asserted for these last two years, is impracticable; to disentangle themselves from the trammels of their own toils, simply impossible. Of any change, however, there is at present no appearance; with a superior degree of art and subtilty the Ministers have made common cause between themselves and the country; they have hitherto succeeded

ceeded in dragging both into the fame labyrinth, and the future condition of this once powerful kingdom is now only to be learnt by an inveftigation of thofe principles that are moft likely to actuate the conduct of its Minifters.

This confideration then is of the graveft import, and it becomes us much, ferioufly to reflect upon the different motives that will probably influence the various fprings that are likely to give elafticity to the future operations of the component parts of the prefent adminiftration.

That terror of innovation, and dread of the extenfion of French principles, have from the beginning of the prefent conteft uniformly guided the policy of Burlington Houfe and its adherents, is a fact that I prefume no one will attempt to controvert. Fear

P   then

then is evidently the cause from which they have acted. The effect it has produced is the war with France. And it of course naturally follows, that, as with the successes of France the original cause will increase, so, as their fears gain strength, their avidity for war must proportionably augment; a dreadful situation indeed, placing us in this singular dilemma, that, when peace becomes indispensably necessary, then shall our executive government be most fixed in their determination to continue the war; when the ability no longer exists of carrying it on at all, then shall we resolve to carry it on with the greatest vigour. As fear acts upon individuals, so must this political terror ultimately act upon the state; for if in attempting to escape a danger we frequently plunge headlong into it, so, upon their own principles, if they persevere in their present conduct, what they regard as the means of

their

their safety must become the agent of their destruction.

Fatal, however, as the operation of this principle must ever prove, by it they have been solely guided, and, true to their fears alone, they first deserted every former connexion, and at length have involved themselves in a situation where the assertion of any constitutional principle would be in itself nugatory and ridiculous. So long as they gave an independent support to government, they might, with consistency, resist any measure they conceived to have an unconstitutional tendency. Their support of the war might be uniform, and their regard to constitutional principles at the same time maintained; but from the moment they went into office, they at once placed themselves in the power of the Minister. To strengthen his hands, to enable him to carry on the war with additional vigour, they came into place; to refign upon their own grounds afterwards is impoffible, in as much as by weakening the executive government they act againft their only remaining principle for which all others have already been abandoned. To affect independence would therefore be abfurd. They cannot be blind to their fituation; they muft feel that the Minifter ftill holds in his hands the powerful means by which he forced them with humiliation into office, and that a repetition of its exertion muft at any time reduce them to paffive obedience.

In the profecution of the war alone, they can have a voice; in every other point, on every other fubject, the mandate of Mr. Pitt muft be the rule of their conduct.

But is this mere fpeculation? Do we not already

already see a complete proof of this position in the difficulty they have found of carrying through the stipulations they made previous to accepting office ? It is needless to enter into the pitiful negotiation for personal honours to be conferred on himself or friends: these, if the Duke of Portland could condescend to bargain for, at a moment of such magnitude, the Minister would naturally and readily grant; it jarred not with his interests, it flattered perhaps his hopes of exposing them.—But let us attend to the great point his Grace is said to have stipulated for—the government of Ireland. That he should feel it desirable and fitting, in the moment of deserting his own political friends in England, to demand a similar sacrifice from Mr. Pitt of his friends in Ireland, is not astonishing: that he who had yielded the uncontrouled sway in Great Britain to the Minister, should wish to posfefs fimilar power in Ireland, is moſt natural; and that he underſtood it to be given up to him, is moſt certain.

How far this ſtipulation will ever be completely carried into effect, it is impoſſible to foreſee : but as the negotiations concerning it have, for months paſt, exhibited one of the moſt ridiculous and diſguſting ſcenes that has, even in the preſent æra, marked the hiſtory of the country[*], ſo

the

[*] It has not been the leaſt entertaining of the many ſingular occurrences that now daily happen, to have obſerved the progreſs of this difference betwixt the Duke of Portland and Mr. Pitt. Their adherents on both ſides have with equal obſtinacy aſſerted, on the one hand that the original ſtipulation was acquieſced in, and the certainty of reſignation, unleſs it is carried into effect, has been publicly avowed : on the other, that the whole has proceeded from miſtake, and the Miniſter's correſpondence with Lord Weſtmorland is brought

forward

the ultimately conceding a reluctant half ſhews in the ſtrongeſt point of view the complete incapacity of the adherents of Burlington-Houſe now to demand or enforce any thing.

From this quarter, then, the country have nothing to expect; in vain do they look for any proſpect of a reſtoration of tranquillity; the operation of alarm is their only ſource of action, and the effect of that
operation
forward to cheer the hopes of his adherents in Ireland. We have ſeen Mr. Secretary Douglas making arrangements for reſuming his ſituation, at the moment another perſon was accepting his place from the Duke of Portland; we have ſeen Earl Fitzwilliam preparing to go, Lord Weſtmorland determined to ſtay. It is now, however, confidently ſaid, that Lord Fitzwilliam is to go, and that Mr. Pitt has preſerved his friends in their ſituations; an arrangement as little calculated to ſatisfy expectant Chancellors, &c. at Burlington-Houſe, as it is to afford a permanent ſecurity for any

P 4 ſubſtantial

operation necessarily involves a disregard and neglect of every other principle and opinion whatsoever.

In contemplating the Minister, and the probable line the motives that have regulated his conduct will induce him to pursue, our hopes are equally gloomy. Guided more, as I have stated at length in my last letter, by personal motives than any other cause, and having succeeded beyond his most sanguine expectation in the object of his solicitude; having divided the party he dreaded; having placed himself at the head of that very aristocracy he originally trampled on,

substantial change of principle in the government of Ireland.—Is it to be supposed that Lord Fitzwilliam can have any real confidence in Lord Fitzgibbon and his friends, or that Mr. Burne and Mr. Keogh can ever receive any boon, however desirable in itself, with complacency from that quarter?

and

and in some degree deserted the cause of those who originally contributed to placing him in power; is it to be imagined he will easily forego what he has taken such pains to acquire, or that he will soon relinquish what he has purchased at so dear a rate?

To effect his original purpose, he sacrificed the peace of the kingdom; and to retain the personal benefit he derived from it, a continuation of the sacrifice is necessary. Great as the price is that one party pays to him, he too must yield somewhat to them. If they sacrifice to him the constitution, he must concede to them the peace of the country. Such is exactly the tenor of their bond—the country between both is totally forgotten; and to gratify the inordinate ambition of one party, to quiet the feminine dreads of another, the obvious interests of

the

the community are to be neglected, our best blood and last treasure expended, and the sad calamities of lengthened war heaped on this devoted nation.

But to this line of conduct other considerations must equally lead the Minister and his friends; for, similar as the contest is in many other points to the American, in this it is most fatally alike—that at the commencement of both we equally out-stepped every fair and considerate bound of discretion, by declaring at once the only terms on which peace could be re-established. There, unconditional submission was to be insisted on; here, the overturning of the Jacobin government is asserted. I speak not now of the supreme folly of the idea in either instance; but I should have thought that the experience of the fatal consequences that attended the practice of it on the former occasion, would have rendered the adoption of it on the latter impoffible.

In the grave hour of confidering the probable iffue of uncertain war, calmnefs and refolution mark the conduct of a wife Minifter; he elevates not his own expectation, or that of his country, beyond the well founded hopes arifing from prefent vigour and immediate exertion; in them he fees the only fource and fure road to returning tranquillity and an advantageous peace; he afferts not what muft depend on accident, but endeavours to act fo as to come up to the expectation of the moft fanguine. Intemperance and paffion form no part of his character, they give no fway to his conduct: unfortunately however for us, whether through miftaken policy or weaknefs, thefe have now for two wars been our

fole

sole guides. In both, the Ministers began where they ought to have concluded; in both, they looked not for success as generating an end, but stated the end to which they were to bring their success; and in both, they, unhappily for the country, early pledged their personal character and reputation to points probably impossible to be attained, and certainly at all events out of the power of man to insure.

The conquest of France, or the counteracting by arms the declared will of twenty-five millions of men in a state of revolutionary enthusiasm, might have appalled the boldest politicians. They, however, in proportion to the magnitude of the object, instead of caution, one would conceive from their conduct, have judged rashness necessary. Pledges were to be made—hopes held out

out to delude and deceive the people, who ultimately, through the vice of the Government and the arts of the Minister, dragged in to support his chimerical ideas, irritated by declamation, and maddened by an appeal to the passions, brought themselves to imagine they saw, in the greatness of the attempt, a sure proof of the talents of the projector—in the vastness of the idea, a certainty of genius adaquate to its completion. Miserably indeed have they been deceived: our ability to carry it on—our Minister's adequacy to conducting it, are now before the public. But the melancholy folly of this our original conduct cannot now be got the better of. Whatever may be our situation, our pride and our honour still urge us forward; our Minister's character and reputation are at stake; and, to save our own and his credit, whatever may now be be our opinion of the impossibility of success, new treasure is to be spent, and more blood spilt.

When in the mind of every thinking man the American war was desperate, what, from the situation in which Lord North had placed himself and the public, was the consequence? New expectation was to be raised, and different measures pursued. This General was to be sacrificed, and some new plan to be adopted. The public hopes were by these means flattered; the people found a temporary relief from the consciousness of their own follies; till at last experience taught them this fatal lesson, that all Generals were alike, that every plan was equally ruinous, the original attempt was in the eye of reason ridiculous, and every subsequent effort proved but the truth of that which wisdom ought at first to have taught them.

At

At prefent, too fatal a refemblance appears; from fimilar caufes fimilar effects are enfuing. Generals may be changed, meafures may be varied; but the ultimate end of the fatal delufion will too furely be found in aggravated difappointment and additional failure.

To carry it on, however, is for Mr. Pitt's perfonal character neceffary; in him every feeling muft lead to the defperate profecution of it: he knows that nothing fhort of ruin can apologize for his treating; and even to the ruin of his country he muft now look for the prefervation of his character and his continuance in power.

But let us not, even in this laft ftage of calamity, flatter ourfelves;—in his confcious incapacity to treat, we may anticipate with melancholy certainty the fure caufe of protracted hoftility;

hostility: the habit of sacrificing principle to convenience may indeed induce the Minister to make a piece of miserable patch-work of his character; but he, and those connected with him, must see that every consideration of policy and wisdom precludes the possibility of his treating with success. The instant he makes the attempt, by analysing his political character as a man, and his conduct as a minister, the whole of our situation will stand unveiled to our enemy. They must know that necessity, not choice, dictates the measure. They must feel that want of ability to carry on the war, and not a wish to re-establish tranquillity, leads to the proposal; they must see that fear of them, and not love of peace, actuates his conduct. In the very proposal they will best discern the extent of their victories; in the past language and conduct of ministers they will alone be able to form a com-a commensurate view of their present strength, and our humiliation. It would be laying the country at the feet of France, and stating in the plainest characters, that any terms must be accepted, because no resistance could any longer be made.

But we cannot suppose the French so blind in their discernments, as not to have marked the political character of the man: it requires not their ingenuity to discover that the depth of his necessitous submission will be proportionate to the extent of his original arrogance and folly. Can we believe for a moment, that they are so lost to the remembrance of even his recent policy, as not to observe, that in the conduct of the wary Empress of the North there is a rule and a guide laid down for their adoption? In treating with him, will they not imagine that it is but to refuse, and new conceſſions muſt be made? that it is only to deny, and freſh ſubmiſſion muſt enſue? The ſacrifice of character, and of what he ſtated to be the intereſt of the nation, *to her*, will inſure the conceſſion of our deareſt intereſts *to them*; and if in the year 1791, to preſerve his place, the Miniſter made light of the honour of his country—when he attempts to treat, in the ſituation to which he has now reduced us, he will learn the conſequence of ſuch conduct, by the ſolid and calamitous ſacrifices he will be obliged to make—ſacrifices not made more to neceſſity, than to his paſt and preſent impolicy and ambition. It will unfortunately, however, not be even neceſſary for them to look back to this memorable event; it is the nature of man to demand what he conceives would have been aſked; and in the ſubmiſſions that Mr. Pitt would have forced upon France, we may form a

competent

competent judgment of the terms that he will have it in his power to make.

Whether then we confider the Minifters in a body, or look at their feparate views as dictating their general conduct, there appears not in either cafe the fmalleft chance of peace; and when we reflect on the futility of the grounds on which they and their adherents maintain the neceffity of war, as it convinces us of their determination to perfevere, fo it fhews equally the perfonal motives and views that actuate them.

In the prefent ftate of things, to hold out even a remote chance of ultimate fuccefs is totally impoffible. *With whom are you to treat?* is therefore the great point to which they refort—wifely, I grant, for their purpofes—though its folution is eafily forced back upon themfelves by the fimple queftion,

tion, *With whom are you at war?* And if there are any to whom this can appear not completely conclusive, let them for a moment reflect *For what we are at war.* Avowedly for the destruction of the Jacobin government of France. The very acknowledgment of our object is then a complete answer to the question. If we once confess that we cannot obtain our end, it involves the natural conclusion, that the dissolution of a government being the end, and it having failed, a government remains with whom we may treat. But our object is stated to be, to destroy, not to form a government. Looking then, if we can, to a successful termination, the fact will whimsically be, that when we have attained the object of our pursuit, then, and then only, shall we be exactly in the situation in which it is now stated to be impracticable for us to treat; and the only time we shall have no-

thing

thing to treat with at all, will be the very moment when, according to the statement of Ministers, peace ought to be made—their object in the war being attained.

Beyond this doctrine of destroying the present government, Ministers have never yet ventured to go : nor for their purposes was it necessary ; for it must be obvious to every one, if they were to succeed in that object, peace could not be made till a new government was formed ;—in its formation, they who destroyed the last must of course have a leading share : and thus, had they succeeded, at the very close of the war, though Ministers from the first never dared to avow their original and true object, it would have ultimately resulted as the natural consequence of the measures they pursued. The farce of overturning a government would be dropped to the ground, and the

the plan of forcing a government on a people ſtruggling for freedom in *their* idea, and determined to be free, would ſtand forward in all its original and native deformity.

But the difguſt naturally excited in every generous boſom by many of the recent ſcenes in France, a horror at thoſe who were the actors on that bloody theatre, and an apprehenſion of a diminution of our dignity as a people, ſhould we treat with a Jacobin Banditti, as it is called, as they contributed to involve us, have, I am well aware, come much in aid of this ſtrange and abſurd difficulty. How far our own conduct may have in part occaſioned the very ſcenes we deplore, and the very horrors we deprecate, I have avoided entering upon; but I ſhould wiſh thoſe in whom humanity takes ſuch a lead, who feel ſo much for the diſtreſſes of a foreign country,

to

to look a little to our domeftic fituation; to confider to what a continuation of the ftruggle muft tend; to think of the effect of increafing burthens; to reflect on the lofs morality muft fuffer; to contemplate the gloomy fcenes the Continent daily exhibits; and then let them decide, whether a fpirit of hatred and revenge againft the French Government fhould in wifdom induce us to be cruel to ourfelves; and whether a deteftation of their barbarity fhould in prudence guide us to ultimate mifery, and poffibly to final ruin.

To thofe dignified perfons who may wifh to facrifice every folid benefit to falfe pride, let me be permitted to put this common queftion—With whom did you treat in the American war? And they muft anfwer with me, —*With profcribed Rebels and a vagabond Congrefs.* Let them go a little further back, and they will find (pride and arrogance yielding

ing to neceffity and policy) the haughty and infolent bigot of Spain, at the very moment of canonizing the murderer of one of the greateft and beft Princes Europe ever faw, forego the object of his early ambition by a virtual declaration of the independence of the United Provinces. Let them reflect that, in both thofe memorable inftances, the language was the fame; ideas fimilar to thofe of the prefent day at both periods prevailed. Let experience be their guide, and let them then determine, whether, to fupport a ftandard of ideal confequence, they are willing to hazard the continuation of the miferies of war, and the bloodfhed of thoufands. But this unfurmountable bar to peace has always appeared to me to originate from a very different, though obvious caufe. Whenever fuccefs became doubtful, the mind was naturally led to look forward to peace; the oftenfible difficulty, *With whom can you treat?* was then artfully brought forward, but

but in reality only as a veil to the real confideration of *Who in this country can treat with advantage to the nation, and honour to themfelves?* Here at once you find a folution of all their clamour—an explanation of the whole of the difficulty.—To keep back this laft confideration, the firft muft be rendered in the minds of the people unconquerable. When once you get over it, the anxiety for peace will be augmented by the road to it becoming apparent; but either the character and confiftency or the power of the Minifter muft be annihilated. To preferve both will then be impoffible; for if the wifh of the people be once with energy expreffed, and he refufes to treat, there is an end of the laft. If he confents to make peace, he bids adieu to the firft: one of them he muft give up. But extinguifh from the memory of all, the paft promifes and pledges; blot from the recollection of the public, the conduct Mr. Pitt and his adherents have

adopted;

adopted; enable them to treat, referving their places and power, with that fcanty pittance of confiftency and character ftill neceffary for public men; give them but the moft diftant opportunity of anfwering the queftion, *Whocan treat?* by faying, *We can*; the weight of the firft difficulty will in their eftimation inftantly fink to the ground; this formidable bar to our happinefs will difappear; and thofe who in the hour of arrogance were ever readieft to calumniate and revile, would, in the moment of ultimate misfortune, be the firft to acknowledge and to treat with the prefent government of France.

In further fupport of this doctrine, a doubt of the exifting rulers in that country treating with you is conftantly infinuated; a point that in all fimilar fituations muft ever remain doubtful till the experiment be made. And why it fhould not now fucceed as as well as in any former war, I own I am at a lofs to fee. That they have anxioufly courted peace fince hoftilities commenced, the public are aware of; and that they would not now treat we have no reafon to fuppofe, unlefs, judging of them by ourfelves, we conceive them to be guided by fimilar prejudices, by the fame averfion to our government that we have profeffed to theirs; and by like interefted motives on the part of thofe who take the lead in the management of their affairs.

But even allowing it to be true, it can be no reafon for not making the attempt: —by that, if made with dignity, we can fuffer no lofs. It may indeed be humiliating to make peace on difgraceful terms; but it never can be difgraceful to offer peace on honourable terms. If it fails, all doubt of the right in the conteft is at an end; it gives us the aid of certain juftice and neceffity, and the

very

very failure will give new strength to our measures—new vigour to our arms.

But this supposition of aversion to peace is in fact another mode of diverting the mind from the impossibility of the present Ministers' offering to treat. It is not the reason of the thing, but the necessity of supporting it for their own purposes, that leads them to urge this preposterous doubt.

Not only therefore the separate and united interests of the Ministers, but the very difficulties they start, must lead us to the melancholy conviction, that it is their desperate determination to prosecute the war to the last extremity. To continue it with success under the present circumstances of things, cannot, I am convinced, be supported by any considerate or reflecting person. It is a dream perhaps reserved for the

warm

warm and juvenile imagination of thofe who have fo frequently anticipated the glory of the Allies in the capture of Paris. With them however I fhall not contend. If they can bring themfelves ftill to credit the poffibility of our carrying on the conteft with a chance of advantage, their inveterate obftinacy may be a matter of aftonifhment to fome: but it muft ultimately be a fubject of grief to all, that, in a time of imminent danger and public diftrefs, the rafh and ill-digefted chimeras of fuch politicians fhould, for a moment, from their perfonal connections, and the fupport they have met with in Parliament, be fufpected to bear any affinity to the matured judgment of the refponfible Minifters of the country.

Of the people whatever may be the fentiments, they will now be but flowly and with difficulty expreffed. Accuftomed ed for years to have a strong party in the country ready to support their interests and to forward their views, in its dissolution they have found, to their cost, the loss of their own energy and of their own strength. They must naturally be diffident in proportion to the weakness of those who support them; and when they look on one hand to the apparent strength of Ministers, on the other to the desperate domestic uses made of it, necessity and prudence equally lead them to be silent.—From the small but steady and concentrated body of men who in either House of Parliament still venture to oppose the measures of the Minister, little can be immediately hoped for. Theirs indeed is a difficult task. Influence, corruption, calumny, fear, prejudice, and pride, are all acting against them in their fullest vigour, and to the greatest extent. Steady, persevering, and determined, they will no doubt

shew

shew themselves to their purpose; but remote and distant is the cure they unaided by the public voice can administer.

There appears therefore no where any cheering gleam of immediate hope, that flatters us with a possible cessation of the present calamities, or gives a prospect of returning tranquillity. When we investigate the feelings and view the conduct of his Majesty's present Ministers, we unfortunately see with great certainty, that nothing but a continuation of hostilities is to be expected: in them, honour, interest and prejudice combine to push on the contest.

For this then we must make up our minds, and it is most necessary we should arm ourselves with fortitude and resolution. Every man must feel, that by this perseverance we risk our own fate; that in endeavouring to
over-

overturn the anarchy of France we hazard the fair form of our own conftitution. Every one muft now be convinced, that the efforts of France are alone to be repelled by means equally powerful.—We may turn the commander in chief of our army into an auctioneer of military commiffions, and fo add to our number when we diminifh the real ftrength of our eftablifhment; we may levy the annual fupply, by entailing beggary and wretchednefs on our pofterity; we may go on debauching the morals of the country by turning the minds of the induftrious to military purfuits; we may continue to encourage unconftitutional benevolences; we may go on addreffing the Crown, and promifing fupport; our Minifters may vent their impotent Philippics in parliament, and mutilated Gazettes may be fent forth to cheer the finking fpirits of the country. But let us not deceive ourfelves. Such and other

other ordinary means will be as impotent, as unavailing. The military character of all Europe already lies proftrate at the feet of French Enthufiafm, and till we employ means fimilar to thofe they have adopted refiftance will be ufelefs. To repel their armies, fimilar armies muft be found; to refift their force, fimilar force muft be produced. Let us therefore not completely fhut our eyes to our real fituation. If war is to be profecuted, to make it fuccefsful French means muft be purfued. Let us not talk of our Conftitution; for before we can act on equal terms with them it muft be, in fubftance, deftroyed; every man muft by compulfion become a foldier; every fhilling of individual property muft become public ftock; our lives and fortunes muft be in a ftate of requifition; and the British Cabinet muft become a Committee of Public Safety.

From such efforts only are we to look for success; but to such, thank God! even Mr. Pitt cannot resort. But are we still to be dragged on, every military judge in Europe having declared the impossibility of success? Deserted by many of those powers originally most sanguine in the cause, are we to continue parrying in the best manner we can the fatal blows of our enemies; consoling ourselves in the ultimate reflection, that a branch of the sea divides us from the Continent; and losing sight of Holland, that miserable country we have ruined with our protection? In this undoubtedly our Ministers may persevere; but if they do, we cannot but suspect they look for their safety to the approach of the melancholy period when all other considerations must be set aside, when all political prejudices must be forgot, when the preservation of our own country must be our sole object; when, to protect our fortunes

fortunes and families, every exertion muſt be made, every human means employed.— Should this melancholy but not improbable ſituation occur, I am completely ready to grant it is no time to ſtart difficulties with whom you will act, or to enter into conſiderations of former political conduct. We muſt all act, and act together; but to learn who is then fitteſt to guide the laſt and deſperate efforts of our country, we muſt neceſſarily turn our eyes to the paſt conduct of Miniſters in their military capacity, and from that determine how far they are to be truſted at a moment when inſufficiency or neglect muſt end in ſealing the fate of this powerful kingdom. If no part of our preſent ſituation be owing to their miſconduct; if all our failures have been the natural reſult of obvious cauſes; if they have been all along the wiſe and watchful but unfortunate ſervants of the public; in that caſe I am

R 2   ready

ready to allow, at a moment such as I have stated they ought particularly to be supported. But if any part of this situation arises from their neglect, if it originates from their folly or want of foresight, we should be committing the worst of suicides any longer to confide in them. And as this is a point of much and deep import to our future preservation, I hope I may be pardoned if I submit to you, with the diffidence due by one not versant in military affairs, a short view of their past military conduct.

There is no failing so great, and at the same time possibly so common in this country, as the inclination we generally feel to undervalue the character of our enemies. The principle from which this feeling arises, however much in itself commendable, has, in its effects, unfortunately but too often proved fatal to our military success; and of this

this the American war is a true but melancholy example. It then actuated alike the army and the senate, our ministers and our generals, our councils and our executive operations. It has recorded in history the British parliament applauding the absurdity of overcoming a continent with a handful of grenadiers *. It occasioned the attack at Bunker's Hill; for to take a fair military advantage of rebels was, by our generals there, reckoned impolitic and unnecessary †.

It

---

* Vide General Grant's speech in the House of Commons.

† It must be generally known that the works at Bunker's Hill were thrown up in one night, on a peninsula. The possession of the pass naturally ensured the surrender of the troops occupying that post, in the course of two days at farthest; and the circumstance of our being enabled to attack it with the tide in our favour, by means of the very boats we afterwards landed from,

It then uniformly guided all our councils; and not even the firſt and ſevere leſſon we received at Boſton could hinder us from attempting the diſaſtrous attack of Charlestown, the ſubſequent expedition under General Burgoyne, or the laſt and deciſive enterpriſe of the Marquis Cornwallis. The hiſtory of that war is a recital of expedients to remedy unforeſeen events; the hiſtory of the government of that day is a tale of accumulated diſappointment proceeding from unfair and arrogant expectation. The miniſters and their generals raiſed an imaginary ſtandard of the energy of the people againſt whom they were to act; and their

gave the moſt complete ſecurity to the attempt. But the appearance of management was ſuppoſed to convey the idea of fear. An inhabitant of America, even behind works, and fighting for liberty, never could be imagined to reſiſt our regular troops. They were attacked in their ſtrongeſt point, and the event is matter of public notoriety.

plans

plans were formed againſt this phantom of their own creation, and not againſt that great, powerful, and temperate continent with which they were contending.

Recent as this example is; deeply as we felt the effects of that ſyſtem of acting; much as it has been deprecated by ſome of the heads of the preſent government, I cannot help thinking that the whole of the conduct of the preſent war ariſes from the ſame fountain; that under-rating our enemies' military character and exertions has been the ſource of all our calamities; that judging of them by an imaginary and not a real ſtandard has been the cauſe of all our failures; and that eſtimating the ſtrength and reſources of the French, not by what they really were, but by what we wiſhed them to be, has been the origin of all our difficulties, and of our preſent ruinous ſituation. In vain may we turn

turn round for any femblance of fyftem or plan fince the beginning of the war; in vain may we look for any appearance of calm deliberation and fyftematic energy in the cabinet:—of hurry and confufion we have fufficient proofs; of inadequate expedients to remedy unforefeen difafters, examples fufficient; but of fyftem or of plan, the bread and ftaff of war, not a veftige is to be feen.

The fituation of the French in Holland at the commencement of the war, might, I am ready to grant, render an immediate exertion for the relief of that country neceffary; and the exigency of the cafe might fairly be allowed to preclude any poffibility of concerting a fixed and fettled plan for the enfuing campaign. Aid was accordingly fent, too trifling indeed to enfure any thing but ruin, had it been the only hope of our ally;

ally: shortly after, however, and most fortunately, the victorious arms of Clairfayt and the Prince of Cobourg drove the French within the limits of their own territory; which was in fact, to us, the fair and legitimate end of one war, and the subsequent operations the commencement of another.

The consideration of what was the surest and speediest mode of making a solid impression in the interior of France, must at this period have become the sole object of military investigation in the cabinet; the necessity of defence was at an end, and offensive measures to be immediately adopted. Here a variety of points were to be taken into view. The nature of our continental connections was of importance to be considered; the real situation of our enemy, and the exact means we had to apply to any given end, were equally points most carefully to be attended to.

The

The number of our alliances at this time muſt, I preſume, have ſolely depended on our wiſh to extend them. All the ſtates of Europe ſaw with jealouſy, moſt with horror, and not a few with fear, the changes that had lately taken place in France; and when they contemplated the military array of Auſtria and Pruſſia in the field, to declare poſitively againſt her was by them too generally, at that time, conſidered as merely giving way to their feelings, and partaking of certain ſucceſs. The ſtate of our enemy, too, certainly held out proſpects flattering in the higheſt degree to our wiſhes. The fate of the unfortunate Louis had already marked the downfall of the timid but enlightened Briſſotin miniſtry; every day they were drawing nearer to their end; and the violence of their adverſaries for a time apparently precluded all appearance of union and combination. The ſeeds of civil war were ſpread

throughout

throughout France, and daily scenes of carnage and murder were for months exhibited in the richest plains of that delightful climate. Their army too was completely disorganised; the despondency of defeat had succeeded to the animation of victory; their favourite General had proved himself a traitor to their cause; all confidence and energy was completely annihilated; even the appearance of an army in the field hardly any where existed. Our own means, it must be allowed, were, as they always have been at the commencement of every war, inadequate to any very extensive scale of operation; but if our troops were few in numbers, they were still formidable from the discipline of the men, and the experience of our officers. Under these circumstances two different systems might have been adopted; the one, to join the British army to that of Prince Cobourg,

bourg, which already with our fubfidized mercenaries was about to act on the northern frontier of France; the other, to have, in conjunction with our fleet, employed the whole of our force on the coaft of France.

The experience of paft wars ought, one naturally would have imagined, to have made in favour of the laft; much and ferious alarm had frequently been given to the French government by expeditions of the kind; and the neceffity of protecting their own fhore has frequently tended to ftop the progrefs of their fuccefsful arms, even in the centre of Germany. The internal convulfions in France feemed to point out the obvious propriety of this line of acting: nor could it be imagined that thofe only would forget to give due weight to this leading point, who were conftantly cheering the

hopes

hopes of the country by inflammatory declamation on this head. Yet such seems really to have been the case. What ought to have stimulated Ministers to an invasion of France had no weight; and, instead of attempting thus to give energy to the opinion of the disaffected, they appear to have come to the resolution of despising all opinion, even when in their favour, and of trusting to the desperate issue of arms only for their success. The smallness of the body of English troops has been stated as a reason for the line they adopted; the insufficiency of the national force, at that period, to any great undertaking formed their principal defence. But it is clear that this is entirely a question of a comparative nature, and here the very smallness of the force appears to make against their position.

That

That a limited fervice can only be expected from a fmall body, muft be granted; but it is alfo obvious, that in an army of a certain magnitude the addition of a fmall corps is hardly perceptible; whereas a fmall corps acting feparately, and with appropriate energy, has frequently rendered effential fervice even to the large army.—The queftion therefore feems to ftand thus: Whether the fmall force that could be provided was of greateft ufe by joining the large army of the Prince de Cobourg? or, Whether, by acting feparately with our fleet, it would not in fact have given greater ftrength to that very army? Whether ten thoufand men hovering or landing on the coaft of France, would not have forwarded that General's views more than they did by acting with him? and, Whether, above all, it would not only have aided his views, but would have tended, if any thing could,

to

to produce a revolution of opinion, from which principally early peace was to be looked for, out of which chiefly returning tranquillity was to be expected?—I would afk too, which way our troops, excellent as I allow them to be, were likely to act with greateſt effect, under the protecting influence of our commanding navy, or as a corps in a German army? Whether as an Engliſh army commanded by Engliſh generals, and acting ſolely for Britiſh intereſts, or as a German corps acting for intereſts by them little underſtood, and poſſibly leſs reliſhed? Whether, in ſhort, from our own troops moſt was naturally to be expected, when the fruits of their victories were to benefit their country, and their laurels to adorn the ſon of their Sovereign; or when the benefit of their labours was to be ſhared by German ſtates, and divided among German deſpots?

All

All thefe confiderations had, however, no effect at this period on the British Cabinet; a different mode of procedure was adopted, different meafures purfued; the moment for fuch an undertaking was forever loft: and though at a future period, and under lefs favourable circumftances, we have been told (with what truth is now pretty clear) the attempt was to be made—ftill, at the time when alone it held out a rational profpect of fuccefs, no fuch meafure was adopted.

It indeed may be matter of well-grounded doubt, whether the rapid fuccefs of the Prince of Cobourg in driving the enemy within their own dominion had not elated the expectation of Minifters to an extent that rendered in their minds all plan and fyftem totally unneceffary; and whether they did not refolve to follow that General's footfteps, as the fure road to eafy conqueft,

and

and to certain fame. Their tone and manner at the time ſtrongly corroborate this idea; nor will the reflecting part of the community hereafter be much aſtoniſhed at the military inefficiency of thoſe Miniſters, who could have the folly and frontleſs audacity to ſtate at the beginning of their career, that the fact of the embarkation of 1900 men of the guards had given a turn to the ſituation of Europe *.

But whether it was occaſioned by the effect of ill-founded expectation of immediate ſucceſs, or whether it proceeded from what I ſhall ever conceive a moſt fatal error in a matured plan, we know the truth to be, that

* It was broadly aſſerted, by high authority, in both Houſes of Parliament, that the landing of the Guards had been attended with the effect I have mentioned; but the fact is, the original victory of the Auſtrians took place previous to their diſembarkation.

the British force in Holland, reinforced from England, joined the allied army, and the offensive campaign against France soon opened by the blockade of Condé, and the siege of Valenciennes. How far this ought to have been made the leading object of the campaign, and whether Lisle would not have been a preferable point of attack, involves a mere military question of detail, into which I shall not presume to enter.

The army had been directed to act in conjunction with the Austrian force. If any blame lay in the conduct of that force (which I am far from asserting), it belonged to the executive officers exclusively, and cannot in any fairness be attributed to our Ministers.

Our object, however, such as it was, completely succeeded. The allied army remained united

united and compact, nor was it long before the gallantry of our own troops, headed by the Duke of York, in pushing the siege of Valenciennes, and the military skill displayed by the Prince de Cobourg in frustrating all the feeble attempts made to throw succour into either place, gave us possession of both these important towns.

But here unfortunately ended, by an immediate change of the system previously adopted, not only the success of the campaign, but of the war in Europe. Hitherto it had appeared to the military officers entrusted with the command of the army, that acting together in one large compact body was the only line by which either security or success could be relied on. They had adopted it at a time when the French army was disorganised and disaffected; nor can it for a moment be supposed, that, in proportion as their opponents acquired additional strength from their increasing numbers, and fresh confidence in new generals, they should deviate from the precautionary wisdom of their former policy.

We must therefore look to some other quarter for this fatal change; and we are naturally led to turn our eyes to the Cabinet of that country which was to derive the exclusive benefit of the measure. It was now the conduct of our Ministers began to appear in its true colour. Infatuated with past success, there was no undertaking too desperate for them to hazard, no scheme too daring for them to undertake. The matured experience of the commanders was disregarded, and to the rashness of their speculations was the success of the war, and the safety of our army, to be sacrificed. They even thought all common official exertion to give effect to the ruinous measures they were concerting, completely unnecessary: and though they must have felt that in proportion to the celerity of the execution the brilliancy of the scheme would appear; though the necessary stores for the siege were meant to be furnished by themselves; yet they were as slow in their preparations to give it effect at home, as they were rash in enforcing its execution abroad. The consequence of such conduct at the time was easily foreseen—the fate of the expedition against Dunkirk was early predicted [*]. Their plan was, however, by the commander reluctantly adopted; the allied army divided; and, after delays of various kinds, as un-

---

[*] I myself heard the officer to whom this country during the present war probably owes most, on seeing the nature of the position the Duke of York was under the necessity of taking, from the inadequacy of his force, predict the event.

pardonable in the executive as in the deliberative character of our Minifters, the events enfued which are of too painful a nature for me to infift upon.

It is not in hiftory to afford a ftronger inftance of the principle I originally laid down. A complete mifunderftanding of the force and energy of their enemy, the undervaluing their means and exertion, muft have led to the deftructive attempt. They have in their defence held out the idea of being overpowered by a mafs, but the fact does not bear them out *. No troops acted againft

* The original decree of rifing in a mafs was prefented to the Convention the 23d of Auguft; the defeat of the covering army at Dunkirk took place the 6th of September. Between thefe two periods it is evidently impoffible it could have been carried into execution, fo as to produce any effect. But the doctrine of mafs is a general apology for all our difafters. How far it is

in

againſt them that they had not grounds to fear might be brought into the field for that

in itſelf true, I have always had ſome doubts. That their armies are numerous we well know; that they have fought with ſuccefs we have all to deplore; but on the long run, I rather apprehend, it will be found that thoſe furious and undiſciplined hordes of Sans Culottes are ſimply large, alert and diſciplined armies, and that their fury is the effect of courage combined with a love of, and a ſenſe of duty to, their country. Allowing it however to be ſo, there is ſurely nothing in it we ought not to have expected. When we view the enthuſiaſm they have diſplayed on every occaſion; when we conſider their general feeling as a people, and their conviction of the nature of the conteſt in which they were embarked; that they ſhould give their money, and offer their lives, cannot be aſtoniſhing. They were only offering a part to preſerve the reſt; they were riſking their lives for what alone renders exiſtence eſtimable. To conceive it involuntary is abſurd, and is contradicted by their uniform conduct in the field, by our total want of intelligence, by their conduct when priſoners, by every practical inſtance that can be adduced.

purpoſe.

purpose. They have attempted too to assert, that even the failure at Dunkirk insured success at Quesnoy and on the Rhine; an idea that cannot require much refutation: for I should humbly conceive no person, but a blind and implicit adherer even to the folly of Ministers, will be found absurd enough to assert it to be a military principle, or even a position that common sense can endure, that, instead of acting on one point in one large body, and against one given object, with nearly a certainty of success, it is wise by dividing our force to attempt two, and to secure the success of one by the calamities of defeat in the other. Yet such was precisely our conduct. Acting in one firm body, as at Valenciennes, against either Quesnoy or Dunkirk, the success of the allies must have been morally certain; acting against both it became obviously doubtful. The rash, nay desperate, attempt

was

was made; the hopes of the campaign were completely blasted: and when the intemperance of the times will again allow calm reason to take her natural sway, mankind at large will join in pitying the ignorance, and despising the folly, of that Administration which could for a moment adopt as a plan, against the most powerful military nation in the universe, the generally dangerous and commonly ruinous expedient of acting by detachment in separate corps *.

* It has been generally imagined this plan originated with the Lord Chancellor, whose deep legal knowledge must be presumed from his situation, but of whose military talents doubts may be fairly entertained. I cannot help regretting, however, that he did not upon this occasion apply to our army abroad, what he must have been well acquainted with, the governing principle of his politics at home; for, if in the division of their opponents Ministers have ever found the source of their own power, he might have naturally concluded, that in the division of our army he was laying the foundation of the power and victories of the French.

But

But let us now trace their conduct in the South, where Toulon, having in common with almoſt every other large mercantile and ſea-port town reſiſted the power and deprecated the principles of Robeſpierre and his faction, and having witneſſed the dreadful example made of other cities, at length reſolved to ſeek for ſuccour and protection even in the arms of their enemies. They had entered into a treaty with Lord Hood, which put him in poſſeſſion of the place; and the French fleet in the Mediterranean, that had ſo long ſwept the coaſts of Italy, had by the ſame agreement fallen into his hands. That the Miniſters here could have no previous conception of the poſſibility of ſuch an event happening, is diſtinctly ſeen from the circumſtance of the equipment of the fleet, in which no military officer of any rank was to be found. Their conduct is therefore only to be conſidered in the

conſequent

consequent steps they adopted after they had heard of the cession of that important place, and this, *in a military point of view*, resolves itself into a very small compass indeed. The only question that could arise, was, whether it ought to be defended or evacuated; and this must evidently have depended upon whether they could furnish the means of an adequate defence.

The melancholy events that subsequently occurred there, explained at once to us their system of acting; and the consideration of the force they might have applied to the defence of that town will evidently shew the folly of their conduct. The defence was instantly decided on, and the means they looked to apparently such as they could draw from Gibraltar, from Italy, or from Spain; for though the usual alertness in Government was immediately displayed in creating ap-

pointments

pointments and wafting public treafure, yet not a fingle regiment of Britifh infantry was fent from England for the protection of the place. The want of men was here however held out as an apology; and certainly it is a valid one, if true. But the want of men, though fubftantial after they had determined to defend it, ought to have come into the original fcale of confideration in deciding upon attempting the defence. Of men, and good men however, there was in reality no want. That army which has fince rendered fuch effential fervice to their country under Sir Charles Grey, and which now unfortunately lives but in the memory of its victories, was ready to act and at hand. To defend this new acquifition in the Mediterranean, they would not at the time give up a projected fcheme of conqueft in the Weft Indies; and though to the plan of invading France, where they had then no footing,

footing, they at laſt ſacrificed this laſt enterpriſe, ſtill they would not ſend a man to Toulon, notwithſtanding our faith was pledged to its ſupport, and every tie of policy and honour alike called upon us to defend it vigorouſly, or to evacuate it totally.

In chooſing a middle line, they ſhewed a want of energy in their military capacity, a want of all regard to faith in their political. In the motley confuſion of their mixed garriſon the fate of the place ſoon became obvious; the loſs of it was a natural conſequence of their meaſures; and the inadequacy and feebleneſs of the conduct of Miniſters, is the only point that ought to excite the aſtoniſhment of the public on the occaſion.

Here again it is obvious how much they under-

under-rated the character and situation of their enemy; a fact still further illustrated by the unaccountable folly of 2000 men having attempted the capture of Martinico in the West Indies—an undertaking that met with the fate its original rashness richly merited.

Such was the conduct of our Ministers in the first campaign; failure uniformly attended all their measures, disaster pursued every step they adopted; and though few could be found of their most sanguine adherents to defend their past conduct, still most looked forward in hopes that the experience they had acquired would serve as a wholesome lesson in future; and that past errors would have so far proved useful, as to have obviated the possibility in times to come of similar principles occasioning similar disasters.

The present campaign then here comes under consideration; and fortunate it would indeed be for the country, could we any where observe the happy effects of dear-bought experience; or could we any how trace in providence, foresight, vigour, and energy, the just return for that unlimited confidence reposed in Government by the nation at large. The history of this year, as far as relates to the war in Europe, is of a nature far too melancholy to be much or long dwelt on. It is a tale of disasters unparalleled in history—it is an accumulation of misfortune beyond the precedent of former days. In this investigation only one point appears to implicate the conduct and character of Ministers; with the late events they could have no immediate interference; these were but military exertions to ward off impending ruin; and, from the capture of Ypres to the present hour, the his-

tory

tory of the campaign is but the journal of a flight.

Previous however to the furrender of that place, it becomes a moſt ſerious matter of difcuffion, how far the Miniſters afforded that aid it was their duty to have furniſhed to the allied army; and whether it was not in their power to have prevented much of the fubfequent difaſter, by early and vigorous meaſures.

The poſition occupied by the French at Menin and Courtray, at the very opening of the campaign, at once preſented a formidable bar to the poſſibility of carrying on offenſive operations till theſe places were retaken. They were accordingly attacked, but without fuccefs. The French in return endeavoured to turn the poſition of the Allies at Tournay; and though they failed to the extent of their expectation, yet the impreſſion they left that day in the minds of their opponents, was of a nature not eaſily to be effaced*. In this ſituation of things then, it was obvious, though the neceſſity of the ſervice was imminent, that the chance of ſucceſs was infinitely doubtful with the force then in the field. To ſtrengthen that army, I muſt preſume, was therefore the duty of Miniſters—to ſtrengthen it ere repeated defeat and diſaſter had rendered even every poſſible reinforcement but an increaſed and ſure prey to the ſuperiority of the enemy. Had Lord Moira's army been ſent to reinforce Clairfayt previous to his repeated defeats, the relieving of Ypres might

* The account given by ſome of the oldeſt officers in the Auſtrian ſervice deſcribes this action as exceeding in fury, obſtinacy, and weight of fire, any they had ever known in the whole courſe of their ſervice againſt the late King of Pruſſia.

T

have

have been possibly effected: by postponing the sending that corps till the first and great issue before that place was completely decided, they rendered it of no real use. Let me not here be understood positively to state, that reinforcing General Clairfayt with Earl Moira's corps would have enabled him to force the covering army at Ypres. This is a military point, resting on documents and knowledge I cannot be supposed to possess; all I mean to say is, that in point of common sense, if that army was ever to serve on the northern frontier, it ought to have been sent with a view to prevent, and not with a certainty of sharing disaster. As it was, its orders were indeed singular. No view of assisting General Clairfayt, no wish to give aid to the Duke of York, no idea of succouring the army, led it to Flanders; but the orders of Ministers to the commander restricted

stricted him to the defence of Ostend—a place notoriously untenable by a garrison, to be defended only by an army in the field. Happily however for our cause, the excellent officer to whom this corps was trusted, by acting from the pressure of the moment, preserved to England a gallant body of troops, now forming part of the army which has of late been retreating from post to post in Holland, at the fiat of General Pichegru; exhibiting on the one hand the ultimate effects of the original military inefficiency of the Ministers, and on the other the deplorable depth of calamity into which a nation may be plunged, when led to support measures adopted not from a matured and well digested consideration of means and force, but from opinions resting on the basis of presumptuous ignorance, generated not by wisdom and provi-

T 2   dence,

dence, but arifing out of folly, vanity, and want of forefight *.

Where or how this will end, it is not for me to decide; let it be determined by thofe who in the capture of the Low Countries, previous to our embarking in the war, faw the deftruction of Great Britain; who in

---

* It has been much the fafhion to introduce the chance of war as an apology for our fituation and a fcreen to our Minifters. In a narrow fcale of military operation it may at times be with propriety urged, but in the extended experience of two years it neither can nor ought to be admitted into our confideration. Thofe too who urge it will do well to remember, that this chance of war, if fo applied, is the greateft of all equalizers; it levels all diftinctions of character and merit; it applies equally to fuccefs and difafters; it alike accounts for the glories of Lord Chatham's adminiftration, and the difgrace of our arms in the prefent.

the

the ruin of the Bank of Amsterdam saw the fate of the Bank of England *.

There are now but few other military points which remain to be noticed. The fate of Lord Moira's army has already been stated. It is not improbable it was originally assembled, more with an intention to amuse the public mind, than from any serious plan of its ever being employed. From the gallantry of the troops, much; and from the character and talents of the commander, every thing was fairly to be expected: but it remains for the ingenuity of the present Government to explain the grounds on which for six months that corps remained perfectly inactive; we being in complete possession of the sea, and Ministers daily vaunting (with what truth is of little

* The language held by Mr. Burke and his associates to urge us on to war.

confequence) the certainty of internal convulfion in France.

In the expedition to the Weſt Indies, fuccefsful as it has fortunately proved, we may again trace the ſteadineſs with which they have conſtantly adhered to their fatal principles. It originally confifted of ten thouſand men: when it failed it had been reduced to half that number. With this inadequate force however, the ability, the enterpriſing ſpirit and indefatigable activity of Sir Charles Grey effected the whole of the object; he put us in poſſeſſion of all the French Weſt India Iſlands: but in this ſituation, though they acknowledged the importance of the conqueſt, they had neither forefight to difcern the probability, nor energy to counteract the poſſibility, of France attempting to repoſſeſs herſelf of thoſe important iſlands. A handful of men got eafy repoffeffion

repoffeffion of the greateft part of Guada-loupe *. Inftead of being re-inforced from home, our Commander in Chief faw himfelf completely forgotten; and at a period when it was neceffary to act with vigour, he found himfelf charged with the defence of all our poffeffions, with a force notorioufly infufficient for the fafety of one of the iflands.

In the Mediterranean we have indeed, at the expence of maintaining for months on that fervice a fquadron that might otherwife have been more ufefully employed, added the kingdom of Corfica to the Crown of Great Britain: but how far the military provifion of Minifters was adequate to the

* It is upon no light or trivial authority I think I can affert that Minifters had intelligence of this expedition foon after its failing from France, though no fteps were taken in confequence.

attempt, is to be afcertained by the conduct of the Commander in Chief*. To the gallantry of our officers and men we here, as on many other occafions, owe much; to the providence and forefight of the Minifters, nothing.

In their management of the navy it is unneceffary for my purpofe to trace much of their conduct: it explains itfelf, and demonftrates its proceeding from the fame principles which have actuated them throughout. Here even the indolence of office could not communicate inactivity to our gallant officers and brave feamen. Where they have been enabled to act, thank God! they

---

* General Dundas is fuppofed to have refigned the command in confequence of a difpute with Lord Hood, who, when he fubfequently applied to the acting commander for military force, was refufed, on the ground of the inadequacy of his numbers.

have yet succeeded, and have fortunately for us still maintained British superiority on its favourite element. It has not been their fault, if our trade has met with an inadequate protection. To them the blame cannot be attributed, that (in sight of our own coast, under the eye of the Minister when at the residence attached to the office he has obtained from a confiding and deluded country) no ship was to be found to keep French gun-boats within the harbour of Dunkirk. That no naval protection was afforded to either our American or East India possessions, lies not at their door. That all the French fleets have arrived with safety in their own ports; that they have been supplied with salt-petre from India, corn from America, and naval stores from the Baltic, cannot be charged against our officers and seamen.

That

That Lord Howe was under the necessity of engaging an enemy superior in numbers, by which the French American fleet got safely into Brest, was not the fault of this gallant officer. His was indeed the well-earned merit of the victory; he needs not the aid of external decoration to make him the admiration of every Englishman. But it remains for the Minister to give a satisfactory account to the public how these things have happened; to inform us why a number of English vessels, which it is considerably within bounds to state as amounting to upwards of 800, are now riding in French ports; how it comes that upwards of 12,000 British seamen are now groaning in French gaols; and how it happens, that at this moment the French are providing for the ensuing naval campaign with stores captured from Great Britain.

I have

I have now, as shortly as the nature of the subject would admit, endeavoured to shew the destructive and erroneous policy that has influenced the military conduct of Ministers: a line still more completely to be ascertained by a concise view of their conduct to neutral nations; not as it regards its justice or iniquity, but as it tends to elucidate the true principles on which they have acted. It would be foreign to my present purpose, wishing only to form an accurate idea of the future confidence which ought to be extended to Ministers in the hour of calamity, by a reference to their past, to enter into a discussion on any general principle of their policy : indeed it would not only be unnecessary, but impossible. No principle to which we may refer can for a moment be supposed to have influenced them, because every different measure the

ingenuity

ingenuity of man could have adopted has by them at various periods been ufed.

Let us look round the Powers of the civilifed world, and there cannot be found, from thofe of the greateſt importance in the general fcale to thofe of the leaſt confequence, a fingle State that has not fince the beginning of the conteſt been infulted by infolent and dictatorial mandates in the hour of fuppofed fuperiority, and which fubfequently has not had an opportunity of thoroughly underſtanding the character of Adminiſtration, by the change of language they have in the moment of calamity adopted. Not fatisfied with aiming at the demolition of the government of France, they ſtruck at the freedom of action of every independent and neutral State in Europe. If France has attempted to difleminate in any public manner

her

her Jacobin principles, they have in a more ſtriking mode endeavoured to maintain doctrines relative to neutral powers, the moſt arbitrary that ever diſgraced the annals of tyranny; they have gone beyond even the junto of tyrants with whom they have been acting; and, to the aſtoniſhment of the world, we have ſeen Britiſh ambaſſadors outſtripping in violence the agents of deſpotiſm.

On examining the conduct of France in the year 1792, we may find much to blame in their treatment of the Italian Powers. Their fleet commanded the Mediterranean, and their meaſures originated from the unprincipled uſe they made of that ſuperiority. Their inſulting mandates were conveyed to the King of Naples by a grenadier, and neceſſity forced him to acquieſce in their wiſhes. In the enſuing year the Britiſh fleet obtained ſimilar poſſeſſion of that ſea, and

and the very reprobated conduct of the French became the example we followed. The Grand Duke of Tufcany was infulted, and the tyrannical exertion of fuperior force compelled him to fubmit. The republic of Genoa, becaufe weak, was oppreffed; the laws of neutral nations were totally difregarded; the confequence of our power was the certainty of oppreffion. In the North our conduct has been dictated by fimilar motives; with this fingle difference, that, in proportion to the fuperior power of the Northern Courts, our commands have been put in a lower tone: but the fpirit is the fame, our fyftem of acting exactly fimilar.

If we look to America, a uniformity of conduct will appear; and though every wellwifher to his country muft join with me in fincerely hoping the exifting differences with that Continent may be happily accommodated,

modated, yet I may venture to assert, without contradiction, that desirable event must be the produce of American moderation, and not of British justice or equity*.

The

---

* If the conduct of France at Naples was unjustifiable, what shall we say to an Ambassador of Great Britain at the Court of Tuscany (acting of course only up to his orders) insulting the Grand Duke, by stating in a memorial to all the foreign Ministers, bearing date May 23, 1793, " that the measures taken with regard
" to the French nation solely and entirely originated
" from the instigations and councils of a single person,
" whose ascendency and power over the mind of his
" Royal Highness could not, from his tenderest in-
" fancy to the present moment, be eradicated." And subsequently on the 5th of October, " The undersigned
" is obliged to declare, in order that his Royal High-
" ness the Grand Duke may be informed of it, that
" Admiral Lord Hood has ordered an English squadron,
" in conjunction with a detachment from the Spanish
" fleet, to set sail for Leghorn, there to act according
" to the part which his Royal Highness may take. The
" unjust and notorious partiality of Tuscany in favour
" of

The character of those who have thus managed the interests of their country displays

" of the French, and the vast seizure of corn and ef-
" fects belonging to merchants of Toulon at Leghorn,
" at a time when the armies of their Britannic and
" Spanish Majesties had occasion for the same articles,
" evidently prove the injury which ensues from such a
" neutrality for the operations of the Allies. In con-
" sequence Admiral Lord Hood declares, in the name
" of the King his master, that if, within the space
" of twelve hours after the representations of the un-
" dersigned, his Royal Highness the Grand Duke does
" not resolve to send away M. de la Flotte and his ad-
" herents from Tuscany, the squadron will act offen-
" sively against the port and city of Leghorn.

" The unhappy consequences of this proceeding
" can alone be imputed to those who have had the
" audacity to give perfidious advice, and to make false
" representations upon the present state of affairs—
" they alone will have to answer for all that may
" happen henceforward."

The papers in respect to Genoa and the North are too voluminous plays itſelf in their conduct in a ſtronger way than I ſhall venture to ſtate it; but when we attend farther to dates, and find we aſcertain the hour of violence and op-preſſion by a reference to our ſucceſs or failure, where can a doubt remain that their judgment has all along been formed by a falſe criterion, their meaſures directed by an erroneous policy?

Nay, even to thoſe of the French for whom they were fighting they have ex-

voluminous to be here inſerted; they are however exactly of a ſimilar nature. Sweden and Denmark have at length emancipated themſelves from our violence by a ſerious armament; and America, after having borne (with a degree of patience exhibited only in a climate where the pureſt patriotiſm reigns, and the immortal Waſhington governs) all our tyrannical proceedings, has inſiſted at length upon an unequivocal explanation of points that both for the honour and intereſt of this country ought long ago to have been ſettled.

U   tended

tended the full conviction of their baneful measures. They never could see expeditions aimed at their foreign possessions, without observing, on the one hand, an application of our force completely foreign from the avowed purpose of the war, and originating from a mistaken idea of the resources of France; and, on the other, a treacherous design of dismembering and ruining what Ministers affected to support. If the sending an army to the West Indies weakened the force you could apply at home against France, the taking possession of those islands gave still greater strength to the rulers at Paris. If, to join the kingdom of Corsica to the Crown of Great Britain, considerable force was similarly misapplied, the very conquest of that island has confirmed the revolutionary government in France.

We have betrayed even the interests of

our

our friends; and the Emigrants muſt view with difguſt, while the Jacobins contemplate with joy, the iniquity of our proceedings.— In ſhort, the policy of Pilnitz has univerſally been ours: the *fides Punica* is the faith of our Miniſters.—We have conducted ourſelves on a falſe opinion of our ſtrength, and of French weakneſs; we have aimed at private advantage more than general good; we have ruined only our friends, and have added to the ſtrength and energy of our enemy. The conſequence of all this, however unfortunate, is but perfectly natural; and as we now ſee the original cruſaders hiding their diminiſhed heads in their German poſſeſſions, ſo are we with our allies, the Dutch, left almoſt ſingly in the conteſt; ſtriking examples of the truth of that approved maxim—That in unprincipled purſuits there can be no concert; between Powers purfuing fuch ends there can be no confidence *.

From

* The authenticity of the following letter, I am well aware, from the nature of its contents, and the high authority it gives to the military doctrines I have ftated, will be attempted to be held out as a fiction. It muft eafily, however, occur to every confiderate perfon, that great impropriety might attend my difclofing the channel through which it fell into my hands. This I muft therefore decline doing; but I may with fafety affirm, from a variety of circumftances, that I have every reafon to fuppofe it genuine that a man can have.

The original is in French; and, in the tranflation, language is a good deal facrificed to precifion.

Copy of a Letter from the DUKE of BRUNSWICK to the KING of PRUSSIA.

" The motives, Sire, which make me defire my re-
" call from the army are founded upon the unhappy
" experience, *that the want of connection, the diftruft,*
" *the egotifm, the fpirit of cabal,* have difconcerted the
" meafures adopted during the two laft campaigns, and
" ftill

From this retrospect of the conduct of the present Administration; from judging by

" still disconcert the measures taken by the Combined
" Armies. Oppressed by the misfortune of being in-
" volved, by the errors of others, in the unfortunate
" situation wherein I find myself, I feel very sensibly
" that the world judges of military characters by
" their successes, without examining causes. Raising
" the siege or the blockade of Landau, will make an
" epoch in the history of this unfortunate war; and I
" have the misfortune of being implicated in it. The
" reproach will fall upon me, and the innocent will
" be confounded with the guilty. Notwithstanding all
" misfortunes, I would not have given way to my incli-
" nation of laying at your Majesty's feet my desire of re-
" linquishing a career which has been the principal study
" of my life: but when one has lost one's trouble,
" one's labour and efforts; when the objects of the
" campaign are lost, and there is no hope that a
" third campaign may offer a more favourable issue,
" what part remains to be taken by the man the most
" attached to, the most zealous for, your Majesty's inte-
" rests and your cause, but that of avoiding further
" disasters?

by the fureft of all criterions, the experience of the paft; thinking as I do of the motives

" difafters? The fame reafons now divide the Powers
" which have hitherto divided them: The movements
" of the armies will fuffer from it, as they have hi-
" therto done: Their motions will be retarded and
" embarraffed, and the delay of re-eftablifhing the
" Pruffian army, politically neceffary, will become
" perhaps the fource of a train of misfortunes for
" next campaign, the confequences of which are not
" to be calculated. It is not war which I object to:
" It is not war which I wifh to avoid; but it is dif-
" honour which I fear in my fituation, where the
" faults of other Generals would fall upon me, and
" where I could neither act according to my prin-
" ciples, nor according to my profpects. Your Ma-
" jefty will perhaps remember what I had the honour
" to reprefent to you the day you quitted Efcheveiler:
" I expofed all my embarraffments, my troubles and
" my misfortunes; I exerted all my efforts to prevent
" any inconveniency: Unfortunately the event has
" proved the infufficiency thereof; it is therefore only
" the intimate perfuafion I have of the impoffibility

" I am

motives that have influenced them, it would be to betray my duty, and violate the truſt repoſed in me, were I, in any ſituation to which either their paſt or preſent infatuation may drive the country, to give to them that confidence which ought, I am ready to grant, to be extended to Government in the cloſing ſcenes of this deplorable tragedy. To act unanimouſly, may, from the nature of

" I am in to effect what is right, which dictates to
" me the meaſure of requeſting your Majeſty to ap-
" point a ſucceſſor to me as ſoon as poſſible. This
" meaſure, however afflicting to me, is neverthelefs a
" conſequence of thoſe ſorrowful reflections I have
" made upon my ſituation. Prudence requires I ſhould
" retire, and honour adviſes it. *When a great nation*
" *like that of France is conducted by the terror of puniſh-*
" *ments, and by enthuſiaſm, an unanimous ſentiment, and*
" *the ſame principle, ought to prevail in the meaſures of the*
" *coaleſced Powers. But when, inſtead thereof, each army*
" *acts ſeparately and alone of its own accord, without any*
" *fixed plan, without unanimity, and without principles,*

" the

of our situation, be desirable; but to act with those whose conduct is best explained by the necessity of that situation, is completely impossible. In the same line of opposition I have hitherto adopted I must still continue—It is a line that may not have met with your approbation, because your view of the subject may have been different; but it is at least one, which in my mode of considering it I have conscien-

" the consequences are such as we have seen at *Dunkirk*,
" at raising the blockade of *Maubeuge*, at the storming
" of *Lyons*, at the destruction of *Toulon*, and at the
" raising of the blockade of *Landau*. Heaven preserve
" your Majesty from great misfortunes! *but every thing*
" *is to be feared, if confidence, harmony, uniformity of*
" *sentiments, of principles, and of actions, do not take*
" *place of the opposite sentiments which have been the*
" *source of all misfortunes for two years past.* My best
" wishes always attend your Majesty, and your glory
" will be my happiness.

" Oppenheim, Jan. 6, 1794."

tiously

tioufly followed, to which I muft invariably adhere, and to which too I am led by a comparative view of the enlarged policy and enlightened underftanding of that perfon who originally ftepped forward, in defiance of calumny, and in defpite of temporary unpopularity, to fave his country from this mafs of calamity. It would ill become me, who confider the friendfhip of Mr. Fox as the honour of my private life, and a fteady adherence to his political principles to be the fole merit of my public character, to ftate to you what might be conceived to arife from perfonal predilection, or a partial political opinion. I feel no hefitation however in referring it to your own wifdom to decide, in calling upon every individual, from the prince to the peafant, to determine, after a due confideration of the refpective conduct of the prefent Miniftry, and of that great ftatefman, whether

the

the talents requisite to save the country are to be found in the enlightened wisdom, in the capacious mind and the prophetic spirit of Mr. Fox, or in the miserable policy, the time-serving expedients and wretched subterfuges of the present Cabinet.

I have now endeavoured to lay before you the sources of my political action at an æra that may truly be said to be not only big with the fate of this country but of the civilized world. I have attempted to explain the grounds on which the Revolution in France happened; to establish that the deadly malady of funding was the disorder, an annual deficit of nearly three millions the complaint; and that in the dissolution of the patient an awful and tremendous lesson to surrounding kingdoms is given; a convincing proof that in public communities, as in individual instances,

" the

" the paths of glory lead but to the grave."
I have attempted to point out to you, that the various component parts of the old regime in France naturally led by progreſſive ſteps to the ſituation in which they now ſtand; and a reference to the paſt experience of hiſtory, a knowledge of the ſufferings they at preſent endure, might not improbably lead us to conjecture, that independent of our interference a revulſion may happen, when individual ſecurity will be eſtabliſhed, and property duly protected.

It has been my wiſh to repel the libellous inſinuation of the probability of a ſimilar revolution happening in this country. Unleſs the oppreſſion of the government be as great, and our financial reſources as exhauſted, the poſition is abſurd. I have endeavoured to ſhew, that no wiſe policy led us to depart from our original ſyſtem of neutrality,

trality, that private intrigue occafioned it, and that public calamity has attended it. I have attempted to explain the evils attending the fchifm artfully created in the Whig party, and endeavoured to eftablifh the impolicy of in future confiding in Minifters, by a reference to their paft conduct.

One fubject I have however carefully avoided entering on. The management of the interior policy at home forms indeed a ftriking feature in the hiftory of the prefent day. We have feen the mild practice of the Britifh law departed from ; obfolete ftatutes reforted to for temporary purpofes ; and temporary conftructions attempted to be given to known and defined laws; much of the friendly intercourfe and relation that fubfifted between the wealthy and the indigent (the beft cement to the ftability of our conftitution) broken down ; the fympathe-

tic

tic spirit of confidence and affection that reigned in the breasts of all, annihilated. A system of *espionage* * has spread abroad a universal feeling of jealousy and doubt: the assertion of conspiracy has divided and disjointed the best energies of our country. The character of the nation has been calumniated, the spirit of the people belied and blasphemed. On this however at the present moment it might be improper to dwell. The impending trials will determine much. Thank God! the lives of our countrymen, and our best interests, are finally to be confided to the solid judgment and impartial decision of an English Jury.

* It is most singular, that to describe the system of the present day, we are obliged to have recourse to a French term. To such a system Englishmen have been so little accustomed, that there is not even a word in their language to convey the idea.

I have

I have now completed my original intention: and if I have defeated the calumnious infinuations that have been thrown out; if I have fhewn plainly and intelligibly the principles I have acted upon, my object is effected. If my language has been ftrong, it appears to me to fuit the nature of the times. I entertain no perfonal animofity againft any man; political conduct is the only fource of my attack. I look not for applaufe, neither do I apprehend cenfure; for I know my purpofe to be honeft, and the execution muft neceffarily be fuch as might reafonably be expected from one who has now certainly for the firft time, moft probably for the laft, endeavoured to attract the attention of his conftituents or his countrymen.

London,
Nov. 1ft, 1794.

F I N I S.

ERRATA.

Page	Line	
26	5	*for* a *read* the
52	13	*dele* that
108	3	*after the word* sterling *insert* annually
145	14	*dele* own
154	5	*for* these *read* the
202	6	*for* or *read* of
245	last	*for* be *read* have been

www.ingramcontent.com/pod-product-compliance
Lightning Source LLC
Chambersburg PA
CBHW030747230426
43667CB00007B/874